RAW
IN
TEN MINUTES

BRYAN AU

Order this book online at www.trafford.com/04-2826
or email orders@trafford.com

© Copyright 2005 Bryan Au.
RAW IN TEN MINUTES
BY BRYAN AU
E-mail: RawBryan@hotmail.com
Website: www.rawinten.com

Bio & Intro Edited by Gail Koffman
Art Direction & Design by Scott Barrie and Kathy Phillips
Photography by Bryan Au
Available on Amazon.com & http://www.RawInTen.com for personal autographed copies

Note for Librarians: A cataloguing record for this book is available from Library and Archives Canada at www.collectionscanada.ca/amicus/index-e.html

Printed in Victoria, BC, Canada.

ISBN: 978-1-4120-5018-0

We at Trafford believe that it is the responsibility of us all, as both individuals and corporations, to make choices that are environmentally and socially sound. You, in turn, are supporting this responsible conduct each time you purchase a Trafford book, or make use of our publishing services. To find out how you are helping, please visit www.trafford.com/responsiblepublishing.html

Our mission is to efficiently provide the world's finest, most comprehensive book publishing service, enabling every author to experience success. To find out how to publish your book, your way, and have it available worldwide, visit us online at www.trafford.com/10510

www.trafford.com

North America & international
toll-free: 1 888 232 4444 (USA & Canada)
phone: 250 383 6864 ♦ fax: 250 383 6804
email: info@trafford.com

The United Kingdom & Europe
phone: +44 (0)1865 722 113 ♦ local rate: 0845 230 9601
facsimile: +44 (0)1865 722 868 ♦ email: info.uk@trafford.com

I would like to dedicate this book to:

GOD for all the love, blessings and miracles that manifest everyday on Earth

And for always loving, providing and caring for all of us!

I would especially like to dedicate this book to and thank "Sunny" Winnie Seto!

This book is only possible because of her enormous loving heart!

She is proof to me that God sends his Angels and this book is only possible

Because of her loving friendship, guidance and support!

Thank you SUNNY!!!

Next I would like to thank my Mom, Dad & family for always loving and supporting me

In wonderful ways always! Thanks My!

I would like to thank Swami Sitamaranada for being my spiritual Yoga Guru

Swami Sita, Swami Swaroopananda and Father Philaret are the most pure and strongest special

spiritual people that I know!

I also want to thank the whole Sivananda Yoga Organization for all of their

Yoga teachings, support and friendship, thank you Siva Kami!

Next I would like to thank all of my clients, especially Lisa Holt & Aaron Porter!

A special thank you goes to Dixie Mahy the Director of the San Francisco Vegetarian Society for

all the truly great work she is doing and for her enthusiastic support.

A special thanks goes to Dr.Laura Lyons for her Raw Living Foods Activism and advice!

Dr. Lyons is one of the most amazing ladies I have ever met!

I want to thank Karen Sussman, Matt Amsden and Peter Kaiser in Los Angeles.

Don Kidson of the Living Lighthouse for his wisdom and friendship!

I would like to thank Alicia Silverstone for being such a super hero Raw Organic Living Foods and

Animal Rights Activist and friend!

I would like to especially thank The San Francisco Vegetarian Society,

The Bay Area Vegetarian Group

Dorleen Tong of the San Francisco Living Foods Group for all of their encouragement, loving

support and friendship. Thanks Wanda and Matthew!

I also want to thank all of my friends and loved ones that all loved and taught me

About life! I am enjoying the journey and still learning!

Thanks Carlos, Jim, Gilberto and Ruby in the Mission in San Francisco!

Thank you to George in Brisbane and Jim Trattner in Santa Monica for helping me be more RAW!

Thanks to Scott Barrie, Connie McCann, Kathy Phillips, from Trafford Publishing for helping me

put this book together!

A final special thank you to Gabriel Cousens, M.D. for all of his Raw Organic Living Foods

research and information!

ABOUT BRYAN AU

I am the founder and CEO of Raw Organic Saving the Planet LLC, an organic raw food and ecology company. Our mission is to create more access, education and awareness about the Raw Organic Gourmet Cuisine and how to protect the environment. It is a company that is meant to heal people and the Earth using traditional business models but in a entirely Raw Organic and Eco way. That is healing everything on all levels from within, using the system to heal itself and to return back to nature. I have found it is much more joyful and more success is gained from working within the system to heal and create positive change. Lets use our collective enlightenment and knowledge to manifest the true joy and peace that we know we can! We already are everyday, it has begun and is getting stronger. It all starts with each individual decision and the great transformation is already happening. I see it everyday in San Francisco, in the media and worldwide. I would like people to know about all the very real Raw Organic and Eco choices that they have and how much happiness, joy and vitality that it will add to their lives. I have seen how people blossom into natural leaders and educators, then they help spread the true knowledge and education to others so that they can all benefit. This is my healing mission and path in this life, but I also want to create opportunities for others on the same path so that we can all grow and succeed together in health, wealth and spirit!

We are in the process of creating a RAW Organic Gourmet Cuisine restaurant, To Go RAW Organic Cuisine franchise, and a packaged food line. I also have Eco housing developments and organic film projects in the works as well. Please e-mail me for investor and business opportunities in these areas. This book is one part of Raw Organic Saving The Planet's overall mission to heal the world and is the direct result of my personal experiences from more than ten years of meditating, practicing Yoga and spiritual world travel.

My journey has taken me to Hawaii, Cancun, Thailand, to ancient temples deep in the jungles of Bourabadour on Java Island and in Bali, churches in London and England, I toured Europe, Asia, the Bahamas, Mexico, most of the 50 United States and Canada. I love Hawaii, Los Angeles, New York and San Francisco where I currently am enchanted everyday by working and living in this wonderful beautiful city. I have studied with holistic and alternative medicine doctors, Chinese medicine doctors, Ayurvedic doctors, and cutting edge organic gourmet raw food chefs. While keeping up with the latest nutrition principles, I have published articles about Yoga, exhibited at art shows, made films and videos promoting charities and fundraisers for many great causes.

Through RAW Organic Cuisine I am manifesting the true spirit of love, joy and compassion as my contribution to healing people and the world. I like to call it bringing "Heaven on Earth." I hope you fully enjoy my recipes in the most healing and healthiest way possible! I engage in constant study of all the modern principles of nutrition and healing from a vast source of experts, most notably Gabriel Cousens, M.D. As the world's foremost live-foods medical doctor, he has authored many well-regarded books, of which I highly recommend that you read. My recipes are based on his incredible research and books.

As a RAW Organic Chef, I create the most decadent gourmet creations as well as all the home style comfort foods and junk food favorites, but with all the benefits of it being raw and organic. This helps people to maintain a raw and organic lifestyle. I am appealing to all the comforts and memories associated with food, so it is not all celery sticks and twigs. Nor is it sushi or just all salads either! It is a highly enjoyable adventure into "super food" and dazzling dining experiences. It truly is the most enjoyable, delicious, most amazing cuisine possible right now on Earth! It has lead me on such great adventures, meeting the most incredible and gifted people while increasing my health and happiness. That is why I created this book so that I can share all this goodness with you.

I started in college studying international business and wanted to change the world for the better, as prescribed in Yogananda's *Autobiography of a Yogi*. He suggested that life is actually a spiritual, healing, loving adventure. Along the way I met some great people and also studied holistic health, that totally changed my world and views on life. Yogananda helped me get on the spiritual path and made me decide to take up the path of healing and peace. That is how and why I began to practice Yoga and found the Sivananda Yoga Center. This lead to my exotic world travels, opening my heart to the world, traveling to amazing places like the Sivananda Yoga Retreat on Paradise Island in the Bahamas. What a fantasy come true! No other experience in my life even comes close to the amazing spiritual awakenings that I had there. It inspired me to use my company name PA~RAW~DISE in memory of Paradise Island, Bahamas and my deep profound spiritual transformations there. I would do Yoga very late at night on the beach and have super realizations about why we are all here and how we should be spreading more healing, peace and love around the world. Being on Paradise Island made every fiber of my being feel so connected with nature and the universe. That is where I first got introduced to organic raw cuisine.

An amazing lady I met from Chicago handed me a flax cracker and I was so interested and curious at the same time. I had never seen anything like it before, it looked like a bunch of seeds stuck together with herbs and spices on top. I tried it and thought it had a great crunchy nutty flavor. When I told her I liked it, she was thrilled and explained to me in detail all the benefits of raw and living food. I was amazed because it was all so new and interesting. At the time I was the vegetarian chef for the Sivananda Yoga Center with over 10 years of professional experience and have been vegetarian since age 12. A whole new world just opened up to me and I wanted to learn all that I could about it.

Since then more and more Raw organic people started to spontaneously enter into my life. Many had fantastic and incredible stories of rejuvenation, miracle healings and life altering experiences. I was so moved by all of their personal stories that I then did my own research by reading all the books I could and going on the Internet. I wanted to find more facts, medical research and conclusive scientific evidence. I became convinced based on my findings and from people that I met that this was indeed the most optimal and incredible cuisine in existence. The best way was through eating it, right away you can tell the difference in the gourmet taste, your energy levels and how satisfied you became by the delicious assortment of new creative foods to choose from. I found that my creativity and artistic abilities were heightened as well as all of my other talents that I did not know that I had. Raw Organic food allowed for more happiness, creativity and greater connections to occur in my life. Then I started to meet even more people and even worked for well known Raw Food Chefs. I trained with the best and eventually connected with Gabriel Cousens, M.D., at his Tree Of Life Rejuvenation Center in Patagonia, Arizona. I have found Gabriel to be the most incredible author, healer and physician on the face of the planet and many people will agree with me. I highly suggest that you read all of Gabriel Cousens's books, I have and they changed my life for the better. I will list more information in the back of the book. Since that time I have been on the adventure of love, light and learning of a lifetime. This book is the culmination of all my life learning and experiences so far. All of my heart, soul and love are literally embedded within each page and recipe of this book. All the support from Angels, friends and family have made this all possible and I am so thankful to God for all of my blessings.

Currently I am a personal trainer, organic raw food chef, yoga instructor, nutritionist, healer, artist, filmmaker, actor, lecturer, consultant, peace activist and CEO of PA RAW DISE. I have worked with celebrity clientele such as Alicia Silverstone, Lisa Bonet. I have clients that are: CEOs, dancers, artists, healers and everyone who is interested in the best, most vibrant health and food on the planet!

It is an honor and joy for me to share the best recipes I can create for you! Life is an adventure and being raw and organic will lead you to greater things in life. Health is the ultimate wealth and I have been telling people that raw will give you more energy and open up your mind to truth so that you can share it with others, help others with support, healing and to just love one another in the best way possible.

Thank you for joining in the adventure,

Bryan Au
Founder and CEO of Raw Organic Saving The Planet
http://www.Parawdise.com
http://www.Rawinten.com

Table Of Contents

Raw Introduction

Welcome to the wonderful world of the Raw Organic Gourmet Cuisine in Ten Minutes! This is the freshest, most creative and exciting new cuisine that is transforming people and the world. It also happens to be the number one growing industry in America today. Celebrities such as Alicia Silverstone, Woody Harrelson, Demi Moore, and supermodels such as Carol Alt all highly recommend organic raw cuisine as the best lifestyle and diet choice possible. Organic raw cuisine is the most delicious, decadent, and enjoyable cuisine on the planet. Now you can easily enjoy and prepare amazing gourmet recipes all under 10 minutes and under $10! I have designed every recipe to be the most balanced, optimal and the best possible for your health, well being and with all natural anti-aging properties.

You should be attracted by the terms "raw" and "organic." After all, our bodies are all raw and organic. So it is only natural that the foods that will give us the most radiant health benefits are foods that are native to our bodies and in nature. This really is the way nature intended us to eat and we have eaten this way for millions of years. The organic raw diet allows our bodies to realign back to its all natural state of optimum health, well being, and vitality. In Yoga we recognize that health, peace and bliss is our very real true self and identity. I like to remind people that real food is from an organic plant or tree.

Most of our reality and present conditions are formed by what we choose to eat. When we eat organic raw cuisine, we are manifesting and creating peace, healing, health, joy, and abundance in the world. Organic food is one of the only few products on earth that is totally healing, nonpolluting, revitalizing, rejuvenating, naturally anti-aging and more. As a result, it makes us youthful, stronger, vibrant, energetic, happier, and joyful. Longtime organic raw food friends have discovered this secret power, which is the ability to make us more beautiful, rejuvenated and youthful. I have found that when you practice Yoga and eat Raw Organic Gourmet Living Food that it is just the best possible synergistic combination and the key to the fountain of youth. You will gain more flexibility, realizations and be able to increase your meditations. All of these wonderful health benefits will motivate you to continue and to go further.

You may have heard glowing personal testimonials about raw food, but there is still much that you have not heard. Although raw food restaurants and products are popping up everywhere, and Hollywood is promoting the raw food trend, you still need to be properly informed. Just because it says "raw organic food" does not make it automatically perfectly healthy. You should still do the research and find out what is the most balanced, optimal Raw Organic recipes and cuisine available as well as what your individual body type and needs are. I have examined the latest medical and scientific research on my own and also based on Gabriel Cousens ,M.D.'s incredible work, to come up with the best most healthful recipes possible. So you can enjoy each and every recipe knowing that they are properly balanced, low in glycemic index or sugar, with proper ingredients for the maximum benefits to your health and well being.

There is new, important organic raw information that I want to share with people and it is based on the vital research of the world's foremost live-foods medical doctor and author, Gabriel Cousens ,M.D. I follow all of his well-researched advice, as he has had great success with thousands of patients and has done the latest medical, scientific and spiritual research on this topic. I have incorporated all of his advice into well-balanced and enjoyable recipes. But my special unique recipes also look and taste like all your favorite cooked comfort and junk foods!

Now it is possible to eat the most enjoyable junk food and comfort foods that are actually the most healthy for you and all in under 10 minutes and $10. You will be able to amaze your friends and family with these easy to follow recipes. You may even think about starting your own Raw Organic Cuisine catering business, café or restaurant using these recipes. I do consultations, training, classes and designing a franchise presently. You will be able to provide the best food on the planet and be offering such a great gift and service to people as well as to loved ones.

All of the recipes are quick. Many of them are totally new innovations that are my original creations while others are more balanced versions of popular favorites and designed to be very simple to prepare. You will find that they are easy, fun, and enjoyable to make. They do not require a lot of complicated equipment, you just need a blender. Nor do they require a lot of prep time. The meals only look like they took hours to make, but all the recipes are under ten minutes! Now you can truly impress your friends and family while providing them with the best loving healing healthy foods available.

We all want to look and feel like a 10. Well now you can! I like to tell people, no time to cook? Great! Go to my cookbook and you will have the healthiest instant meals possible. They all look like you spent hours in the kitchen creating the most gourmet meals, but they all take ten minutes or less to make. Many are my most closely guarded secret recipes and innovations. So many people have thanked me for sharing my secret recipes and have asked me to publish this book. That is why I am willing to share the best of what I have with the world.

The saying "You are what you eat" and also Hippocrate's "Let thy food be thy medicine and thy medicine be thy food" is so very true. But with this book, we take it to an all new level with the most enjoyable, delicious, vibrant, colorful and organic gourmet raw food on Earth.

Whether you are new to organic gourmet raw cuisine or a dedicated raw foodist, you will love this book and all the recipes because they are literally the best and easiest on the planet. All in under 10 minutes and $10!

RAW IN TEN MINUTES
extreme HEALTH
Wild Tibetan
GOJI BERRIES
THE HIGHEST RATED ANTIOXIDANT (ORAC) FOOD IN THE WORLD
As seen on TV
Compare Antioxidants
Food | ORAC Units
Goji Berry | 25,300
Prunes | 5,700
Raisins | 2,830
Spinach | 1,260
Brussel Sprouts | 980
Broccoli | 890
Oranges | 750
Cherries | 670
Exclusively used in Chef Bryan Au's Book "Raw in Ten Minutes"
Our Goji Berries are gathered wild in Tibet, sundried, are not fumigated, processed or artificially sweetened.
(NET WEIGHT)16 OZ.

Chapter 1

One of the main points of the Raw Organic Cuisine is the fact that everything is 100% Organic and Raw! Being Organic puts this cuisine above the rest simply because it is so pure and natural. Our bodies are also 100% Raw and Organic, so it only makes perfect sense that we consume the same thing. All the effects of Organic Fruits and Vegetables are so healing for people and the planet. This is what attracted me to this amazing special cuisine at the beginning. You will also discover that it allows for so much creativity and joy in your life too. I look forward to creating new recipes everyday. It is such a rewarding fun experience for me to be able to create new awesome recipes for people to enjoy. I want to really urge you to do as much research as you can on why you should support and consume Organic products. It is one of the most valuable of all things on Earth that is all natural and totally environmental. With that said ALL of the ingredients in this Recipe Book are 100% Organic and RAW. I wanted to state that because I did not type Organic and Raw in front of each and every ingredient but do want to emphasize this major important aspect of the Raw Organic Cuisine. Sometimes this very important concept is overlooked when it should be emphasized. There really is a difference, once you eat more Organic food you will notice how much better you feel and won't want to go back to inorganic food. Sometimes people ask me if Organic is too expensive. I tell them that they are worth it. There are no pesticides used in the food, the water is very pure, all of the land and workers are protected. There are many strict beneficial standards that are met when food is certified to be Organic. The truth is all the goodness that they will get in their health and in saving the Earth is worth the slight extra cost. Also the more we all support Organic fruits and vegetables the more mainstream and profitable it will become so the prices will go down for all of us. That is why I am trying my best to promote organic and raw living foods. I would like it to be normal and mainstream again. Not too long ago food was already all natural and organic and we did not have to even label it as being organic, times have changed but one day I hope that we can return to that natural state of being and living. The intent of this book is to introduce new people to this wonderful new cuisine and also to offer the advanced Raw Foodists with the best Raw Recipes in the world. Everyone will love how fast, easy and fun all of these under 10 minutes and under $10 recipes really are. The Raw Organic Cuisine is really taking off as there are movies like Woody Harrelson's *Go Further* which I highly recommended that you go see and support, more exciting vibrant Raw Organic Products, books and restaurants popping up everywhere. This is such a beautiful trend. It is currently the #1 growing industry in America. So thank you for joining in the adventure and I hope you truly enjoy all of my recipes to the fullest.

Next is the difference between Raw and Living Foods. Raw foods are those that are not cooked and in their natural state. Living foods are still alive, growing and vibrant. People like to explain that living foods can be put into the earth and a plant or tree will grow as a result. Raw food can be sundried or dehydrated, but none of my recipes use dehydration so you will save a lot of time and energy. The food will not lose any active enzymes or nutrients while being able to add more water and hydration to your body. Our body is made of over 80% water so the more pure water you drink or get from food the healthier you will become. My recipes are tantalizingly juicy and moist which will help keep you hydrated and at peak performance levels while being super delicious and gourmet.

Some examples of living foods is sprouts, fruit, and nuts that are soaked overnight. This is one of the few things that take time in prepping. But it is simple and easy so don't worry. Whenever it says "soaked" in front of an ingredient or item it means that you should soak that ingredient overnight with bottled glass water in a large covered bowl or container in a clean dry area. This will make the Raw Food turn into Living Food that is alive with enzymes, life force and nutrients very much in the same way as your body. Enzymes are the building blocks of life and the secret to the fountain of youth. Raw Living foods has the highest amount of enzymes possible so by eating these recipes you will be increasing the amount of enzymes in your body which will help increase your energy levels, naturally anti-age and give you strength. By soaking ingredients, using sprouts and miso along with many other techniques that I have incorporated into all of my recipes you will be able to deliciously enjoy all the super benefits without even realizing it and become super heroes! That is what makes my recipes so special and you can be assured that you are getting the best. A lot of new information and research has been done most recently that other recipe books may not have incorporated. There are always new exciting research and discoveries being made everyday so it is important to stay up to date with the most up to the minute information.

Some items only require a few minutes of "soaking" like Tibetan Goji Berries or Sundried Tomatoes but I will specify that in each recipe. If it just says soaked then it means soaking it overnight before you go to bed, which is very simple. You may also soak the same ingredients for another day or two if you want them to be sprouted, you just have to change the water and rinse often and be sure that it is in a dry clean area. Often times we can convert Raw foods into living foods by soaking them in pure water overnight and allowing them to sprout or be activated. In all of the Recipes in this book you may choose to use the nuts as Raw or Living by soaking them in pure water over night. Soaking the nuts makes them easier to digest and they then do become living foods. You can interchangeably use Raw or Living nuts just remember that soaked nuts are wetter in consistency and that you should drain and rinse them very thoroughly before using.

Now I would like to describe the equipment that you will need to make these recipes and also the ingredients that we will be using often throughout the book. I designed these recipes to be the quickest, most economical and fastest possible but with the most gourmet and decadent flavors too. Again it is for the total beginner and also the Raw expert. So we will mainly be using the Blend-Tec blender, measuring cup, a vegetable mandolin, sharp knife, vegetable grater, peeler and cheese cloth. You can also use a food processor for some recipes if you want the consistency of certain ingredients to be finer or powdered but the Blend-Tec blender is perfect for all of the recipes. Blend-Tec blenders make the food deliciously smooth, creamy, more enjoyable and very easy to digest. It is also a very fun piece of equipment to use and is required for all of these recipes! I have used just about all the different kinds of blenders out there and although you can use a very inexpensive one to make these recipes, you really should invest in the best one possible since they are heavy duty so will last a very long time, are strong enough to perform and it shows in the quality of the food that you will be preparing. It also pays off in having a Blend-Tec blender because it makes the food easier and more fun to prepare. Out of all the blenders that I have used in all the different kitchens, I prefer and can only recommend the Blend-Tec Blenders! They truly are the "Rolls Royce" of blenders. They are quiet, smooth, computerized with nice lit up digital LCD displays with easy to use soft push buttons. Many of them also have a 3 horsepower motor so they are very strong, sturdy and the blades are made of the highest quality aircraft grade stainless steel. Their jugs are light, easy to clean and the food does not hide or get stuck behind the specially designed blades like with other blenders. In my opinion they are truly the best in quality, design, craftsmanship and I truly enjoy using my Blend-Tec Blender so much that I am more than happy to recommend it to you.

Sur La Table has the most unique kitchen items and gourmet products to dazzle you, I truly look forward to all of my shopping experiences there! I also buy a lot of kitchen equipment and supplies at Rainbow Grocery in San Francisco. All the plates, glassware and kitchen supplies that I buy are all from Rainbow Grocery and Sur La Table in San Francisco. I shop at Rainbow Grocery a lot and just love everything about them. I feel so good in supporting and knowing that there are other like minded aware people, like at Rainbow Grocery, that have chosen to have the best business practices and organic products for people to enjoy.

Now that you have the equipment, I want to let you know where the best places are to buy organic fruits, vegetables and nuts. First I would recommend your local Organic Farmer's Markets as they have the freshest and best selections. In San Francisco the Ferry Building is really promoting Organic Produce and they have a very good selection while the location next to the Bay is very beautiful. Just ask the locals when and where the best Farmer's Markets are and they will tell you, San Francisco is a very social and friendly city. You can also get to know the farmers on a nice personal level and get great discounts. Organic Farmers are doing us such a great service by really taking on the extra time and cost to lovingly provide us with the best that nature and God have to offer. They really deserve our support and it is so fun to shop at Farmer's Markets. But not everyone has access to a Organic Farmer's Market and they are not always open around the clock so I also often shop at Rainbow Grocery in San Francisco, Trader Joe's, Whole Foods and Wild Oats. Rainbow Grocery is so unique and special because most of their products and offerings are high quality 100% Raw Organic with good prices and they also do not sell any meat or animal products other than cheese and honey! So I shop there the most and highly recommend that you do too if you live in San Francisco or are visiting. Next is Trader Joe's, I love their prices and selection of Raw Organic Fruit and Nuts. They really have great deals and are making a serious effort to carry more Organic Products so we should support their very noble efforts. Whole Foods and Wild Oats is pretty awesome for Organic foods too with good quality selections and can be found in most areas. Again the more we support Organic products the more profits these stores can make and so their buyers will order more organic selections and soon the prices become better for everyone and it becomes a winning situation. Even regular super markets are beginning to carry more organics so try to only buy organic! The more you practice this the more other companies will have to transform and cater to our needs. We can make a positive difference and each choice we make really counts. I personally only buy organic and environmental products, it makes me feel so good knowing that I am supporting people and companies that are really doing it right. I also love the fact that they are providing me the opportunity to be able to treat myself to the best organic benefits for my health, well being, the environment and the world.

Now I will go over the list of ingredients that we will use the most in this book. I will also explain what their benefits are. I am even introducing new super foods like Organic Tibetan Goji Berries. They have the highest amounts of antioxidants, vitamin C and are full of super goodness. They also have a wonderful natural happiness inducing quality about them. Whenever I eat a handful I feel energized.

It is so much fun for me and an extreme pleasure to provide the best, most healthy super food for everyone to enjoy and bliss out on. These are true blessings of health, wealth and spirit and it is such a joy for me to help show people and to promote and introduce Tibetan Goji Berries as the next big thing and super food because they are so incredibly amazing and tasty! Also with my recipes please note that they are all really well researched and formulated to bring you the maximum amount of health, rejuvenation, anti-aging properties and are all based on Gabriel Cousens, M.D.'s researched principles. There are many ingredients that I will not use and others that I promote fully. But I have found that most people do not really like to be told what they can and can't eat so I have to recommend that you read ALL of Gabriel Cousens' books as they are all the best and have the true medical, scientific and spiritual information about the Raw Organic Cuisine. I am so thankful for Gabriel's research and contributions to the Raw Community. I even e-mailed the Nobel Committee in Switzerland to nominate him for a Noble Prize! I feel his contributions and achievements to the Raw Living Foods community and world is that great. I will leave it to his expertise to explain to you what ingredients to avoid and which ones to use. Just know and realize that in this book I have done the best research possible to bring you the fastest, most gourmet and enjoyable RAW Recipes in under 10 minutes and under $10, but they are also the most balanced and the best for your health.

Some recipes may go over the 10 minute mark but only by a little and as you practice you will become really good and you will also be able to prepare them faster. Some recipes only literally take a few minutes or less then 5 minutes. The number one thing is to be able to enjoy the experience while being safe. I just wanted to remind everyone that the under 10 minute concept is not a race or requirement but an estimate of how long these recipes take to make. But I want people to enjoy the process and not rush or hurry to make that 10 minute mark! If you take your time you will find it to be so fun, rewarding and relaxing. For me it is like a meditation and total ZEN experience because I am so in the moment fully concentrating and enjoying what I am doing. All while knowing that I am preparing the best food possible on the planet! This is the way we ate for millions of years and the way nature intended. All of the 6 billion living beings on Earth eat and thrive on raw organic food. This is definite food for thought and an interesting figure. We are only now starting to learn more from nature's wisdom and rediscovering all natural healing and lifestyle choices. That is why we should become more environmental and protect the same nature that provides for our needs so abundantly.

Also some recipes may go over the $10 mark but most are well under $10 and the ones that may go over are a lot less once you calculate the cost of making the individual servings. All of the recipes are created to serve 1 to 2 people and I will state if a recipe goes over that so you will know that you will have extra servings. It is always good to have some extra Raw Organic Food in the refrigerator on hand so that you can just reach in there and enjoy it later or to share with friends and family. You can of course double or triple the recipes accordingly if you have more guests or people to serve. With ALL of these recipes you should eat and serve them right away for the maximum amount of freshness and nutrients, but then please cover and refrigerate everything right away so that the food will be protected and last a long time. With all foods you should cover and refrigerate what is not eaten or is left over. I like to use the Pyrex brand glassware because they are so sturdy, attractive and easy to use. I buy all of my Pyrex at Rainbow Grocery and you will see them in the photos.

Most of the food should last several days to 1 week maximum in the refrigerator, please use your common sense and compost the food if you suspect that it is no longer fresh. You will find that some of the Raw Organic Food will actually taste better with some time because the ingredients and flavors get a chance to meld, mix and merge for even more flavor. But for the maximum amount of energy, enzymes and nutrients try to eat it right after preparing. Also please carefully wash everything very well before preparing any recipes, this includes your hands, all equipment, utensils, plates, kitchen, etc. Use all natural organic eco soaps and cleaners like the 7th Generation brand or similar eco products with biodegradable packaging. Each choice you make really does affect 7 generations into the future! So lets make our collective decisions and future brighter with our awareness and positive choices. Cleanliness is next to Godliness and we are striving to be the best that we can. Please wash the produce and your hands often before and during food preparation.

You will be able to totally amaze your friends and family with the incredible creations from these following recipes. And even the complete beginner with very little skills in the kitchen will finally be able to amaze people! Back to the ingredients list, remember to make sure that it always says RAW and Organic on the produce/label/jar/bulk bin/etc. They are listed in the order of being used the most in the recipes. I buy most of them at my local Farmer's Markets and Rainbows Grocery but will list where else you may find them.

Pine Nuts: I like to use these because of their creamy smooth flavor. They come from pine cones! Also their small size makes them really easy to blend. They make the best creams, sauces and are also great whole. I sometimes will mix them with Tibetan Goji Berries and have an instant super food trail mix. The best Pine Nuts at the best prices can be found at Trader Joe's. Rainbow Grocery also carries them in their refrigerated section, at Whole Foods and Wild Oats they will have them in their bulk section, make sure they say Raw Organic on them. I like Trader Joe's because they are individually packed and retain a great fresh flavor at the best price. If you can find them even fresher at a Farmer's Market then I would say go for that. Always try to taste them first to see how fresh and good they are. Each crop is different and you want the best.

Brazil Nuts: These only grow in the Rainforest and have amazing healing properties in them. I have found that they make the best Alfredo Sauces and go well in some desserts too. If you like you may sometimes substitute recipes that say Pine Nuts with Brazil Nuts and Brazil Nuts for Pine Nuts, you can experiment on your own later to keep things fresh, new and exciting.

Almonds: These should definitely be sprouted and soaked overnight in the most pure water you can find. They have so many health benefits and more are being discovered each day! We will be making

Almond Milk and also be using the left over Almond Pulp a lot in many recipes so it is important to get some good quality all natural cheesecloths. You can drink the almond milk or store it in glass jars for later use. The pulp should be used right away or be stored in glass Pyrex containers in the refrigerator. The Almond Milk Recipe is in the Raw Oatmeal and Cereal Recipe. On the Internet I found information that states that Raw Almonds have healthy fats, have been found to help reduce heart disease and also help people lose weight when they are on low calorie diets with raw almonds. They are very high in anti-oxidants like Vitamin E and are high in magnesium.

Sunflower Seeds: These are the most affordable out of all the Raw Organic Nuts and some recipes only require sunflower seeds. They are easy to blend because they are already small in size and they can be used instead of other nuts in some recipes. They can also be soaked overnight and sprouted before use. They are very versatile and also happen to make the best sprouts. I love the way they taste and how they come from giant beautiful flowers.

Olive Oil: I use this special ingredient in most recipes because of its great flavor, energy and for natural health reasons. There are many different types of Organic Olive Oils on the market today. I like to use Bariani which is worth the extra cost or Olive Oil from Greece that Trader Joe's carries is very reasonably priced. In Greece olives and olive oil is a very spiritual ancient tradition and practical religion, they even have purity laws in place for olive oil producers! I have found that olive oil from Greece is very balanced, neutral in PH with a nice creamy flavor. Their technique for producing olive oil is as close to being raw and living as you can get. You may want to try different brands for fun and variety, just make sure they are all cold pressed extra virgin organic olive oil.

Sunflower Sprouts: I like to use New Natives brand, it says Sunflower Greens Organically Grown on the package. They are very high quality and their Website is: Newnatives.com. Gabriel Cousens, M.D., says that sprouts is one of the best Raw Living Foods you can eat and I believe him. Sprouts contain vital living enzymes, nutrients and yes they are still growing! I prefer Sunflower Sprouts because of their flavor, presentation and because they are so thick that they last longer than other sprouts. I use them in a lot of recipes and people love it. You can of course sprout your own but they take several days to do so. I will refer you to books about sprouting in the Recommended Books Section in the back of the book. Sprouting is a very fun and rewarding experience, it will connect you with the miracles of living foods and the forces of life. I just prefer to buy them already sprouted for convenience. They go very well with most foods and recipes, taste great and are very versatile living super foods.

Maine Coast Sea Vegetables Kelp Granules with Cayenne Pepper: The Maine Coast Sea Vegetable brand is awesome as they magically blend these two ingredients together in one package for you which saves you time. It says Sea Seasonings and Organic Kelp Granules with Cayenne on the package. Their Website: Seaveg.com. I have also heard David Wolfe say in his lectures that you should use kelp granules often because you will supply your body with all the minerals that it needs and craves. In Ayurvedic Medicine it states that cayenne pepper activates the digestive system and promotes healthy digestion of food. It also adds a nice spicy flavor and "heat" to the food. So on a cold day or during the winter you may want to use more cayenne pepper in your food. I use it in most of my recipes but it is optional for you according to your liking of spiciness. They also sell whole Dulse in a 2 oz. Package, it is like a vegetarian version of "ham" and "bacon", I have a friend who likes to just eat them whole as a snack out of the bag.

Cold Mountain brand Hawaiian Mellow White Miso, South River brand Azuki Bean and Chickpea Miso: I use Miso in most of my recipes because Gabriel Cousens, M.D., recommends using Miso over other traditional salty soy products. Gabriel really goes in depth as to why in his new amazing book: *The Rainbow Green Live Food Cuisine* which I recommend that EVERYONE must read. All of my recipes are based on his incredible research and analysis. I am so thankful to Gabriel for his dedication to promoting the best Raw principles in a medical, scientific and spiritual manner that is fun and easy to read. Gabriel also talks about how Miso can help us avoid certain kinds of radiation problems in his books. I notice that tons of people now use cell phones, everywhere you look they are glued to people's heads! Well the reality is these cell phones give off a certain amount of radiation and even when not in use. I do not use them. But if you do, eating Miso may help to alleviate and prevent certain health risks associated with radiation. Again Gabriel is the doctor and goes in depth about it in his books. There is also a lot of information about the dangers of cell phones on the Internet and the possible cancers or traffic accidents that they might cause.

I love the flavor that Miso imparts in the recipes and food. It adds depth and energy to all of the recipes and Cold Mountain is made in the USA, is Kosher, very organic and is unpasteurized so is considered a living food! It is the only none Raw product in this book, but is considered to be living food because of the active living enzymes. It has no cholesterol, is low fat, contains isoflavones and is gluten free. You can find it at Rainbow Grocery and most health food stores as well as Whole Foods and Wild Oats.

When you read the label and description for the South River brand of Miso you will be so amazed at all the care they put into it. First I totally appreciate the extra thick glass jar they use for extra purity and their entire process is just one of the best! It is the only one that is handcrafted in the centuries old traditional Japanese farmhouse technique. They say that each teaspoon contains millions of active enzymes which unlock the nutrition and full flavor of all foods. We will use their Azuki Bean and Chickpea in many of the recipes. Their Website: Southrivermiso.com. These are the ONLY 2 miso brands that I use

Sea Salt: I only use and recommend the Original Himalayan Crystal Salt, it is so superior in every way and is truly the best. We all deserve super spiritual food and high quality healthy ingredients. I love the crystalline shape, high vibrational energy and super flavors in each delicious grain of Original Himalayan Crystal Salt. It is the only brand of salt that I will use in my special Raw Organic Cuisine preparations and the only brand I recommend. It is such a pleasure for me to let people know what is the best and the Original Himalayan Crystal Salt is definitely that and much more. After reading the Website: http://www.originalhimalayancrystalsalt.com, you know you are getting all the super benefits and you also get to enjoy the super flavor while knowing that you are getting the best salt in the world. This is such a blessing and gift. Thank you Original Himalayan Crystal Salt! So to get my recipes perfect and just right only use the Original Himalayan Crystal Salt brand. You can order directly through me or at my PA~RAW~DISE Raw Organic Cuisine Restaurant on Union Square in San Francisco. Please visit as we do have special RAW Tour packages and you will be able to enjoy the best Raw Organic Cuisine that is designed to be the most delicious, satisfying but also the most optimal and healthy on Earth.

RAW Organic Agave: I wrote RAW Organic because many brands are not Raw and Organic so make sure it says that on the label! Agave is vegan and comes from a cactus native to Mexico. It also has a very low glycemic index or sugar content level and yet it tastes so amazingly sweet. I love its texture, color and flavor. Other even lower glycemic sweeteners is stevia, the powdered version takes getting used to but the liquid form is very good. I only use and recommend Madhava Raw Organic Agave in all my recipes and food preparations. Madhava Raw Organic Agave is the best quality, price and is available everywhere, their website http://Madhavahoney.com.

I use Agave as a sweetener in my desserts and smoothies. Diabetic friends and clients have been encouraging me to promote liquid stevia more and have reported great success with using it for their sweetener. I have a lot of information and recipes specially designed for diabetics that I have been wanting to promote and make more mainstream for people's benefit. In many ways the Raw Organic Cuisine has so many proven balancing and healing properties for Diabetics, please e-mail me for more information. There is a lot of new Raw Organic information that will help them eat and live in a more enjoyable delicious balanced way. Order the BEST Liquid Stevia from 1-877-989-9954. I only use and recommend Super Stevia. It is the best and please tell them Bryan Au sent you!

Fresh Young Thai or Mexican Coconut: We will be using these very often in many recipes. Be very careful when opening. For the safest technique PLEASE place the coconut on a sturdy table or surface that can withstand a lot of pressure. With a large heavy sharp knife, a butcher knife being the best, hold the handle firmly and make strong firm chops on the top of the coconut and form a square in order to open the top. IMPORTANT: Make sure NO one is around you within a 10 feet radius because you have a very sharp knife in your hand making chopping motions and pieces of coconut will fly around. Also NEVER put your hand near the coconut when chopping it! I have seen people hold the coconut while trying to chop it open and I have heard too many stories of people cutting themselves and do not want that to happen to anyone! So please be safe and just follow my instructions when chopping a coconut open, so the best way is to chop a square "lid" on top, after each chop put the knife down and then turn the coconut so you can make another chop that is 90' degrees perpendicular so that eventually you will make a square that will become a lid that you can lift open and get to the coconut water and flesh. In recipes that call for the coconut water just pour it into a bowl and take out all coconut fiber and particles out before putting into the blender. Also NEVER put your hand into the blender even if you think it is unplugged or turned off! It is ALWAYS good to be safer than sorry, this is especially true and important in the kitchen. If you are not careful or fool around you can create serious harm and injuries that may not be fixed and can be very severe. I just want to remind everyone to be safe and aware. The kitchen is a very fun creative place but please always use caution and common sense to get the maximum enjoyment out of your experiences.

If the recipe does not call for coconut water but for coconut flesh, you can just drink it or put it in a glass jar and store in the refrigerator to use later. When scraping the coconut flesh or meat out, use a large spoon but then also scrape off all the debris, coconut splinters and fiber off of the coconut flesh and meat before using in the rest of the recipe. Be really careful to get all of them out because they do not blend, taste, or digest well at all. Please make sure that no splinters, fibers or hard pieces of coconut shell make it into your blender. Young Fresh Coconuts from Thailand are good but are not always organic, the best organic ones come from Mexico. In some recipes if you do not have access or can't find any fresh young coconuts then you may substitute it with almond milk or grow your own coconut palm trees!

San Benedetto, Panna, Glacier, Fiuggi and Evian Water in Glass Bottles: I only use these waters in my food and recipes. Not only are they ultra gourmet and pure but they make the food taste great. Please never use tap water in these recipes! These bottled waters ensures the maximum amount of purity and I love how they come from protected sources. San Benedetto is an artesian well water from the base of the Alps in Italy and is my favorite at the moment because of the quality and they also have a recloseable cap. I also really like the overall flavor of San Benedetto. Fiuggi is also a favorite of mine, it is a low mineral content water and on the label it says that for several centuries it has been the favorite of artists like Michelangelo and of Popes, their Website: Sangemini.com. Be careful to choose the still or non-carbonated waters, although you can use the carbonated version, the still water is much better and what we will use.

The other brands of waters are really great too but make sure they are all in glass bottles because plastic bottles leach small amounts of plastic into the water! Remember we are trying to make the most pure and best high quality gourmet food on the planet. You deserve the best! Filtered water is ok but if you do not change the filters often enough then you can get a build up of germs and bacteria in the water and also things can come off of the metal or plastic pipes so make sure you change the filters often and have good plumbing. I just prefer and recommend using gourmet glass bottled water. Please recycle all the bottles after using them! All of my clients appreciate that I use the best quality water possible.

Organic Tibetan Goji Berries: These have not caught on in America yet but I am doing my part to promote them as one of the best all natural healthy super foods and snacks you can eat! First they are sundried so have absorbed super energy, then they have built in super nutrition. There are many websites that are also promoting them. Some of their amazing health benefits is that they have the highest amount of anti-oxidants, they have 500 times more vitamin C per ounce than oranges, have super amounts of vitamin: A, B1, B2, B6 and E. They have more beta carotene than carrots and in certain studies have been found to have anti-aging and anti-cancer properties. Please use this special link to make purchases online at: http://www.Extremehealthgoji.com or call 1-800-800-1285.

Nutiva Organic Extra Virgin Coconut Oil: I love the Nutiva brand because of their high quality and value. I use their coconut oil in many of my desserts. It is like an all natural pastry cream! But with tons of good natural high quality fat, it has no cholesterol in its raw form and it is not a trans fat. You can put it in your hair for extra shine, eating it will bring out the natural beauty from within and it tastes amazingly great. I use it in my totally innovative and unique dessert recipes like the RAWeo and RAWinkies. It is awesome in pies and smoothies, is naturally sweet, creamy and delicious. Their Website: Nutiva.com.

The other ingredients that I use like Organic zucchini, limes, carob powder, etc. are pretty common and easy to find just make sure they are ALL RAW & ORGANIC. Just to be sure once again ALL the ingredients in all of the recipes MUST BE RAW & ORGANIC. There an important list of why you should support Organic in the Why Choose Organic section in the back of the book.

Some good kitchen and equipment safety: When using a mandolin or grater be extra careful not to cut yourself! The blades are very sharp so please be very careful not to slice the veggies or grate them too close to the blade where you might cut yourself, it is very easy to forget this and don't rush these recipes, take your time and enjoy the process they are all fast easy recipes so there is no hurry. Please be very aware and conscious of what you are doing when you prepare the food and recipes. The relaxed, focused, meditative thoughts and feelings that you have will be absorbed in the food so don't try to make these in a hurry. I even know people that will consciously pray for health, wealth and abundance over the food while preparing it and they notice a very increased positive experience, energy and taste in the food when they do so. We can always use all the blessings we can get! So please exercise common sense and also if you ever drop a knife take a step back and don't try to catch it. Always wear closed toes shoes to protect your feet and to keep from slipping, no slippers or going barefoot in the kitchen or prep areas please. I want everyone to be as safe as possible and to enjoy the best experience possible as well.

Since this is a self published Raw Organic Cuisine Living Foods book, photos of the recipes are on the cover of the book and I will state which recipes correspond with which photograph. The photos and recipes are in different order and there isn't a photo for each and every recipe on the cover. However there will be color photos that you may print and view of most to all of the recipes on my Websites and you may e-mail me to make your experience interactive!

I have 3 Websites and you may always e-mail me with questions, advice, business, to book lectures or book signings, consultations and classes. They are:

http://www.Rawinten.com

My e-mail is: Rawbryan@hotmail.com

With all of that said lets get started and have some fun!

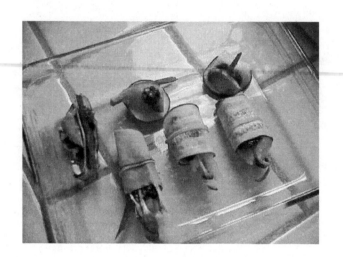

APPETIZERS

RAWvioli

Dim Sum

Honey Dew Melon wrapped in "Prosciutto"

Endives Stuffed with "Tuna Fish" and "Salmon"

Bruschettas

Pizza Boats and Mini Pizzas

Nuggets with BBQ Sauce

Spinach Dip

Curried Hummus

Pita & Lettuce Wraps

RAWvioli

*T*hese are a very creamy, easy and delightful start to any meal. If you are having a party, entertaining or have an event you don't want to spend too much time preparing food and want to socialize as well. Well with this book you finally can! The RAWvioli make a perfect appetizer and are an elegant sophisticated yet simple way to start things.

For 2 to 3 Servings

"Pasta":
1 Peeled: Jicama or 1 Zucchini or 1 Butternut Squash

Filling:
1 Cup Pine Nuts
3 Large Basil Leaves
Finely chopped Rosemary
2 Tablespoons Hawaiian Mellow White Miso
¼ Cup Water
Sea Salt to taste

Peel the jicama or zucchini or butternut squash then carefully use the Mandolin to create very thin slices. Put these slices on a plate and cover with olive oil or better yet truffle oil from Trader Joe's (these are a seasonal specialty item).

In the Blend-Tec blender pour in the water first then all of the filling ingredients then blend until smooth and then put into a bowl.

Cut the thin slices of jicama or zucchini or butternut squash into either circle, rectangular or square shapes. Start to spoon small amounts of the filling into the center of each shape then fold the jicama or zucchini over so that the circle becomes a half moon RAWvioli, the rectangular shape becomes a square and the square one fold diagonally to form a triangle. Drizzle with more olive oil or truffle oil if available. Garnish with chopped chives on top and finely chopped rosemary.

Variations: Keep some left over Pine Nut Filling in the Blend-Tec Blender and add more water to make it into a liquid sauce and blend. Pour over the RAWviolis. You can also add some tomatoes before blending to make a creamy tomato sauce. Or use the Marinara Sauce from the Hawaiian Pizza Recipe and spoon over the top and drizzle with more olive oil or truffle oil and enjoy!

Dim Sum: For some Dim Sum you can use the RAWvioli Recipe and use the "Tuna Fish" and "Salmon" recipe from the Endives Stuffed with "Tuna Fish" and "Salmon" Recipe in the jicama and zucchini slices. They both look like rice wrappers that they use, you can also add some grated carrots and small bits of red bell pepper for extra color and flavor inside. Use sesame oil instead of olive oil and you can make dipping sauce by mixing South River Azuki Bean Miso with some water.

Honey Dew Melon wrapped in "Prosciutto"

A quick Italian favorite. Now vegan raw and organic! It looks and tastes just like the none vegan version that you will really be surprised! You can place the slices on a bed of crushed ice if you will be leaving it on a buffet table or for a party. It is also a great way to eat whole Dulse and get great minerals.

4 SERVINGS

½ Honey Dew Melon cut into 4 slices and peeled

1 Package of Dulse by Maine Coast Sea Vegetables Company,

Website: Seaveg.com

Olive Oil

4 Fresh Cherries or Strawberries

4 Mint Leaves

4 Toothpicks

You really need the Maine Coast Sea Vegetable Company's Large Sundried 2oz. Dulse for this recipe because their Dulse is the highest quality and the perfect large size as well. Get the Dulse from the package and scrape off the excess natural sea salt to taste. Then dip the Dulse in a plate of olive oil and cover the Dulse in olive oil then wrap the Dulse around the middle of each Honey Dew Melon, assemble a large mint leaf, cherry or strawberry on top and skewer into place with a toothpick and serve.

You will find that the Dulse will look and taste like "Prosciutto" and that the whole large Dulse is very much the all natural vegan "ham" and "bacon". You will be getting some serious living enzymes and nutrition from the Dulse because it is sundried and has a good source of protein, iron, chlorophyll, Vitamin A & b, more dietary fiber (33%) and soluble fiber (16%) than oat bran and is super pure since it is certified Organic by OCIA International.

Endives with "Tuna Fish" and "Salmon"

I came up with this "Tuna Fish" for a client that wanted a no mercury pure Raw Organic Version. This recipe is so creamy and delicious just like you remember and love. Now you really get to enjoy more. The same holds true for the "Salmon".

MAKES ABOUT 10 SERVINGS

2 Endives separated into individual pieces

"Tuna Fish":
1 ½ Cups Cauliflower Tops
½ Cup Walnuts
½ Lemon juiced
¼ Cup Water
2 Tablespoons Hawaiian Mellow White Miso
Sea Salt to taste
Dash Kelp Granules with Cayenne
Finely Chopped Rosemary

"Salmon":

1 Cup Grated Carrots

¼ Cup Pine Nuts

¼ Cup Water

½ Lemon juiced

2 Tablespoons Hawaiian Mellow White Miso

Sea Salt to taste

Dash Kelp Granules with Cayenne

Finely Chopped Rosemary

Place the separate Endive pieces on a serving platter or tray.

In the Blend-Tec Blender put all the ingredients for the "Tuna Fish" in starting with the water first, then walnuts, cauliflower. lemon juice and the rest of the ingredients. Blend until smooth yet still chunky and spoon into a bowl and then into the endive pieces.

To make the "Salmon" put the water into the Blend-Tec blender first then the pine nuts and all the rest of the ingredients, blend until smooth yet chunky. Spoon into a bowl then into the endive pieces.

You can use small pineapple chunks, small chopped cherry tomatoes, or sliced olives for garnish.

Bruschettas

In certain regions of Rome, Italy a meal has not begun until the Bruschettas are served. Luckily that should not take long with this easy recipe.

2 to 3 Medium to Large Heirloom Tomatoes
Olive Oil

Choice of Toppings:
"Tuna Fish"
"Salmon"
Guacamole from the Spanish Lasagna Recipe
RAWvioli Pine Nut Filling
"Ground Beef" from the Taco Recipe
Olive Spread from a jar or your own blend
Choice of finely Chopped Rosemary, Cilantro, Mint and Basil for garnish
Sliced Olives and chopped Tomatoes for garnish
Sea Salt to taste

Fill a plate with medium slices of Heirloom Tomatoes cut into wheels. Drizzle with olive oil. Then spread different Toppings on top, drizzle with more olive oil and garnish with sliced olives, chopped tomatoes and sprinkle some finely chopped rosemary and add finely chopped basil, dash of kelp granules with cayenne on top and serve.

Pizza Boats and Mini Pizzas

These pizza boats and bite sized mini pizzas are made with zucchini so are crispy and crunchy. They are very festive and colorful. They are the perfect quick snack and party food.

About 25 Servings

4 Zucchini

Olive Oil

Sea Salt

Marinara Sauce from the Hawaiian Pizza Recipe

RAWvioli Pine Nut Filling

Sliced Olives and chunks of Hawaiian Pineapple (optional) for garnish.

Finely Chopped Rosemary and Basil

Cut 2 of the zucchini in half lengthwise then scoop out the seed and middle to form "boats" put on a plate, slice the other 2 zucchini into thin wheels and drizzle all the zucchini with olive oil on top and sprinkle sea salt. Fill the boats with the marinara sauce and spoon small amounts of top of the zucchini wheels. Drizzle a little more olive oil on top then drizzle some RAWvioli Pine Nut Filling on top(optional) and then use the desired garnish. Top with the finely chopped rosemary and basil.

Variation: You can use the "Nacho Cheese" Pine Nut sauce instead of the RAWvioli Filling. The "Nacho Cheese" Pine Nut sauce is from the Tamale Recipe.

Nuggets with BBQ Sauce

*E*veryone loves dipping nuggets into a nice BBQ sauce. One of my surfer friends would call good waves in Hawaii "Nuggets". That was his way of describing something really good and that is a good description of this party favorite. There is even a Raw Ketchup and Sweet Mustard Dipping Sauce too!

MAKES ABOUT 12 SERVINGS

1 Cup Ground Golden Flax Seeds

1 Tablespoon Raw Organic Tahini

3 to 4 Tablespoons of either: South River Chickpea Miso or Cold Mountain Hawaiian Mellow White Miso

Chopped Rosemary and Basil

5 Tablespoons Olive Oil

2 Tablespoons Water

Sea Salt to taste

Kelp Granules with Cayenne Pepper

Finely Chopped Basil and Rosemary

Ground the golden flax seeds in the Blend-Tec blender until a fine powder. Then mix with all the other ingredients in a large bowl. Form desired nugget shapes with your hands or with cookie cutters. Kids love to help make this recipe, you can make all sorts of fun shapes.

Raw Ketchup

A̲n all raw organic version of your favorite sauce in the world. Very satisfying and refreshing.

2 Tomatoes chopped
¼ Cup RAW Apple Cider Vinegar
¼ Cup Soaked Sundried Tomatoes
Dash of Agave
Sea Salt to taste

In the Blend-Tec blender, blend all of the ingredients and pour into a serving bowl.

BBQ Sauce

For BBQ Sauce blend Raw Ketchup with some South River Azuki Bean Miso and Agave to taste! Pour into bowl and serve. Kids and adults alike love this one and the kids can help you make it.

Spinach Herb Dip

A nice creamy dip for all your favorite raw organic veggies. You can use this as a spread or even put a little on top of a soup for garnish and for a creamy touch.

7 Servings

2 Cups Baby Spinach Leaves

1 Avocado

1 Cup Cilantro or Parsley or a combination of both

Finely chopped Basil and Rosemary

1 Tablespoon Curry Powder or Turmeric

1 Tablespoon Hawaiian Mellow White Miso

1 Tablespoon Tahini

Sea Salt to taste

Kelp Granules with Cayenne to taste

¼ Cup Water

Pour the water first into the Blend-Tec blender, then seed the avocado and scoop it in, add all the other ingredients and blend until smooth. Serve with raw organic green and white asparagus tips, on heirloom tomatoes, purple cabbage leaves cut into triangle shapes, sliced radish, fresh pea pods and yes even carrot and celery sticks.

Spinach and other raw organic greens helps to alkalize the body's Ph. The more neutral to positive Ph your body is the healthier and more optimal it becomes. A balanced and well researched raw organic gourmet recipes definitely helps you to accomplish this naturally with the most enjoyable dining experiences ever! Each bite becomes a celebration and adventure into "super food" as you are helping to bring more "Heaven on Earth."

Curried Hummus

People often ask "Where do you get the protein?" well besides nuts, avocados and olives, which are all high quality proteins and fats, chickpeas also provide a great source of protein. Especially when they are sprouted and soaked overnight. Hummus is a very creamy versatile type of dip and spread. It goes with practically everything.

7 Servings

2 Cups Soaked Chickpeas
½ Cup Tahini
1 Grated Carrot
Some Purple Cabbage Leafs
Some Red Bell Pepper pieces
Sea Salt to taste
1 Teaspoon Curry Powder
Kelp Granules with Cayenne
¼ Cup Water

Pour the water into the Blend-Tec blender first, put all the rest of the ingredients in and blend until smooth.

Pita or Lettuce Wraps: Use red lettuce leafs, chard leafs or romaine lettuce and spread the curry hummus down the middle of each leaf. Add sliced avocado, sliced olives, chopped tomatoes, cubed cucumbers, sunflower sprouts, drizzle with olive oil and enjoy! You can use the Pine Nut Sauce from the Falafel Balls Recipe.

Variations: You could also use sundried nori wraps, or sushi seaweed sheets is the more common name. Find the sundried variety as most are toasted or roasted. The sundried have all enzymes and nutrients intact. The Eden brand has one of the best organic sushi seaweed sheets from protected oceans. You can roll the curry hummus in them for a quick snack, some people even will use the sushi wrap then use lettuce leafs either outside or inside then roll them to make an quick interesting fresh wrap. You can call it a curry sushi wrap! You can also use the Spinach Dip Recipe to wrap things up too.

ENTREES

Hawaiian Pizza

Deep Dish Pan Crust Pizza

Spanish Lasagna

Pasta Alfredo

Angel Hair Pasta

Pasta Marinara

Cheese Tortellini

California Rolls

Dim Sum

Tamale

Macaroni & Cheese

Taco

Burrito

Tostada

Super Nachos

Pad Thai

"Steak"

Nut Loaf

Mashed Potatoes & Gravy

Home Style Pot Pie

Sun Burger with Fries

Burger Buns

Sloppy Joes

Chili Cheese Fries

Island Kebobs

Samosa

Calzone

"Chicken" and "Turkey"

Holiday Stuffing

Falafel Balls

Oatmeal and Cereal

ENTREES

Hawaiian Pizza

America's #1 Favorite food is the well loved Pizza! Well here is a great Hawaiian version that will please all Pizza Fans. This Hawaiian Pizza is perfect for picnics, parties and large events.

The Deep Dish Pan Crust is a hit and doesn't need any baking, just a few minutes and you are done! This gives you more time to enjoy your celebration and be social or to savior your Pizza.

2 SERVINGS

2 Pieces of Chard

2 to 3 Roma Tomatoes

4 Sundried Tomatoes soaked 10-30 minutes in water

¼ Cup Olive Oil

¼ Cup water

Several sliced Olives

Organic Hawaiian Pineapple from Maui

2 Tablespoons Hawaiian Mellow White Miso Paste

Kelp Granules with Cayenne Pepper

Sea Salt

Some fresh Basil and Rosemary

Sunflower Sprouts

Figs(optional)

Quick Pine Nut "Cheese":

1 Cup Pine Nuts

¼ Cup Water

2 Tablespoons of Olive Oil

Sea Salt to taste

In the Blend-Tec blender, pour in the water first then add the sundried tomatoes, miso, olive oil, Roma tomatoes, a few dashes of the Kelp Granules with Cayenne Pepper, several pinches of sea salt, some finely chopped Rosemary and Basil then blend to desired consistency longer for a smooth blend and shorter for a more chunky quality. Then spread onto well washed Chard leaves the size of a personal pan pizza. Next put all the ingredients for the Quick Pine Nut "Mozzarella Cheese" in the Blend-Tec Blender and blend until smooth. Add chopped olives and pineapple chunks, sunflower sprouts, chopped figs(optional), some finely chopped basil and rosemary. The best and most refreshing Pizza in under 5 minutes! The kelp granules gives your body all the minerals it needs, the cayenne pepper helps increase digestion along with all the enzymes in the Pineapple. The figs add color and look like pepperoni or sausage. It is also a great way to get more greens such as chard which most people do not get to eat enough of, it will create a positive and very alkalizing PH that will keep you young and looking great. Makes 2 pizzas. This is a very gourmet and pleasing favorite among my clients, family and friends. You can even experiment with different "crusts" like purple cabbage, lettuce, kale, let your creativity and imagination shine.

Deep Dish Pan Pizza Crust: that really looks and tastes like a baked greasy pizza, ground 1 Cup of golden flax seeds by blending in the Blend-Tec Blender until a near fine powder. Put in a bowl, add 2 tablespoons of water, 2 Tablespoons of olive oil and dash of salt to taste, mix very well and spoon half the mixture on to a plate, this will make 2 deep dish pizza crusts. Then using a fork form a triangular pizza crust and pat it down so it stays together. Then pour the above tomato pizza sauce, pine nut cheese sauce and put the toppings on it. You can drizzle more olive oil on top for that "greasy" pizza! With this crust you will need to use a fork to eat the slice of pizza since it won't stay together if you try to pick it up with your hands. For the "ham" you can use Maine Coast Sea Vegetable brand Dulse. If you cut it into certain shapes it looks and tastes like "ham" or "bacon." You can even use it to make a Raw BLT if you put the Dulse in between some lettuce leaves, sprouts, tomatoes, the above pine nut cheese sauce. This Hawaiian Pizza Recipe looks and tastes just like a baked greasy pizza and there is a photo on the cover.

Spanish Lasagna

Nothing can be faster or easier than this unique festive recipe. This one really looks and tastes super gourmet. Many people new to Raw Organic Cuisine tell me this one tastes so "cooked" or "baked" that it amazes them and they are surprised when they find out how quick it is to prepare. This recipe gets people so enthusiastic and motivates them to get into Raw and to learn more. I have had so many people decide to really go Raw after trying this wonderful easy recipe. It is super creamy and delicious too.

4 SERVINGS

- 2 to 3 Avocados
- 2 Zucchini
- 2 Roma Tomatoes
- 4 to 5 Pieces of soaked Sundried Tomatoes for 10-30 minutes in water
- 1 Lime
- 1/2 Lemon
- ¼ Cup Water
- Kelp Granules with Cayenne (optional)
- Fresh Basil and Rosemary
- Sea Salt
- Yellow or Red Bell Peppers
- 2 to 3 Tablespoons Hawaiian Mellow White Miso
- Olive Oil
- 1 Cup of Brazil Nuts

What makes this recipe so special is how very quick and easy it is to prepare. It looks like it took you hours to make this gourmet entree but should only take 10 minutes! People love its creamy festive textures and flavors. First use a vegetable mandolin to make thin slices of "pasta" with the zucchini. Then marinate on a plate with drizzled: olive oil, lime juice, sea salt, then place into a 7" x 7" glass pan and make a thin layer across that is slightly overlapping when they meet.

Guacamole: will make this dish super creamy and Spanish! Seed the avocados, spoon into a bowl and mash in a bowl with a few squeezes from the lemon, add some sea salt, 2 tablespoons of miso, some finely chopped rosemary, several dashes of the kelp granules and cayenne pepper, add chopped Roma tomato, sliced olives then mix with a fork into the desired consistency of Guacamole. Then spread the Guacamole on top of the zucchini layer in the glass pan. Squeeze a little more lime juice on top and add some more chopped Rosemary and Kelp Granules then layer more thinly sliced marinated zucchini on top to form another thin layer. Now add water first then tomatoes, some chopped basil and rosemary, soaked sundried tomatoes, olive oil, sea salt, 2 heaping tablespoons of miso paste, into the blender and blend until smooth. Then pour and spread over the layer of thin zucchini that you just made in the glass pan.

Next we will make the "Ricotta Cheese" with the Brazil Nuts! Add ¼ Artisan Spring Water into the blender, add the Brazil Nuts, a few squeezes from the lemon, sea salt, fresh finely chopped rosemary, 3 to 4 dashes of olive oil then blend for 2 to 3 minutes. Then pour small amounts on top of the marinara sauce and make it look like clumps of cheese over the top. Then add fresh small whole basil leaves and sprinkle more dulse granules and cayenne pepper on top and you have the world's best and fastest Spanish Lasagna. It is so creamy and delicious I always get a lot of requests for this one and it is a huge favorite at RAW Classes and demonstrations. It also makes a great entrée for a café or restaurant. There is a nice photograph on the back cover, it is in a Pyrex glass pan with the Buddha in the background.

Pasta Alfredo

This one is also a super favorite at RAW Classes and restaurants alike. People are amazed at how quick, easy and delicious this recipe is! It motivates them to go further and to go Raw! This recipe is so refreshingly delicious it is easy to see why.

2 SERVINGS

2 Zucchini
Olive Oil
Fresh Rosemary and Basil
Dulse Granules with Cayenne Pepper
Sea Salt
Hawaiian Mellow White Miso
2 cups of Brazil Nuts
1 cup of Spring Water
Lemon
1 Roma Tomato
Sliced Olives

Use the mandolin to create thin slices of "pasta" then use the knife to carefully cut "pasta noodles" then marinate with a squeeze of lemon, olive oil and sea salt and let sit for 5 minutes.

"Alfredo Sauce": In the Blend-Tec blender add water, several squeezes of lemon, Brazil Nuts, a few dashes of sea salt, 2 tablespoons of Miso, some finely chopped rosemary and then blend until smooth. Adjust the water and olive oil to desired consistency. Then pour over the zucchini noodles and add chopped Roma Tomatoes, olives and a dash of olive oil and sea salt, sprinkle a little dulse and cayenne pepper, add more chopped fresh Basil and Rosemary and other favorite veggies, enjoy!

There is a nice photograph of the Pasta Alfredo on the cover, it's on a blue cobalt plate with the Buddha in the background.

Angel Hair Pasta

*T*his Angel Hair Pasta is so quick and colorful. The Yams make up the Angel Hair "Pasta" and it literally gives off a vibrant glow. The decadently creamy smooth sauce plays well off the flavor of the yams. Pasta lovers will be so delighted.

2 Servings

1 Large Yam or 1 Butternut Squash

1 Cup Brazil Nuts or Pine Nuts

½ Lemon

Fresh Basil (optional for a Pesto Sauce)

¼ Cup Olive Oil

2 Tablespoons of Hawaiian Mellow White Miso

Sea Salt

¼ Cup Water

Kelp Granules with Cayenne Pepper

Diced Tomatoes and sliced Olives for garnish

This is a really quick tasty meal and it looks very gourmet! Peel the Yams then using a fine grater try to use long even strokes to get the longest Angel Hair like consistency. Carefully place the Angel Hair Yam "pasta" onto a plate. Drizzle with olive oil and squeeze lemon juice on top.

Now make the Pesto or Alfredo Sauce for the topping. In a Blend-Tec Blender first pour the water in, add the nuts, olive oil, sea salt, miso, squeeze more lemon juice then blend to desired consistency, 2 to 3 minutes for a thicker sauce and longer for a smoother finer sauce, add Basil if you want it to be a Pesto Sauce.

Pour the sauce over the Angel Hair Yam Pasta, add the diced tomatoes and sliced olives and sprinkle the dulse granules and cayenne pepper on top and serve! It is a very colorful festive entrée in just a few minutes. You can also use other sauces on top of course, like the marinara sauce, you can create a pineapple miso sauce and make it Hawaiian, use your creativity and imagination.

Pasta Marinara: You can also substitute the yams with zucchini, grate the zucchini and add marinana sauce from the Hawaiian Pizza Recipe mix and serve. You can add "Meat Balls" by using the "Ground Beef" recipe from the Taco Recipe, just roll and compact using your hands into "Meat Balls."

Cheese Tortellini: Peel the zucchini then carefully use the Mandolin to create very thin slices. Put these slices on a plate and drizzle with olive oil. Cut zucchini into rectangular shapes. Start to spoon small amounts of the "Nacho Cheese" Pine Nut Sauce from the Macaroni & Cheese Recipe, filling into the center of each then using your thumb and forefingers "pinch" both ends then fold up the middle so both ends meet at the top and it will look like tortellinis. Drizzle with more olive oil or truffle oil if available and serve.

California Rolls

These are really quick fun "Sushi" Rolls that are Vegan and will totally amaze your friends! Instead of Nori or Seaweed I use thinly sliced Yam and Zucchini for that unexpected new twist and flavor. These California Rolls and "Sushi" are the most refreshing and amazing tasting! They look very artistic and gourmet and are a crowd pleaser. I even had a California Roll Party where I invited some friends over and we spent the whole time making California Rolls, Sushi and also Dim Sum with left over vegetable pieces.

About 12 Servings

2 Large Zucchini or

2 Yams

Purple Cabbage Leaves

Pineapple from Hawaii

2 Haas Avocados

Azuki Bean Miso from South River

South River Chickpea Miso

Papaya from Hawaii

Sunflower Sprouts

1 Carrot

Using a Mandolin carefully make thin slices of both zucchini and yams and set aside. Next cut the pineapple into small chunks about 1 inch long and ¼ inch wide. Scoop out large chunks of avocado and papaya and set aside.

Now place the chunks of pineapple, small slices of avocado and papaya(looks like salmon!) on top of one end of the zucchini slice and also on top of one side of sliced yam. Put a little of your choice of Miso just on the top rim on the pile you just made, then put 1 to 2 sprigs of sunflower sprouts on top so it is sticking out above the top. Now carefully roll them into California Rolls. With the Zucchini you will find that it is easy and sticks together well. With the Yam you may have to use some carrot "string" to tie it together so it does not unravel after you roll it, you may also use this for the zucchini rolls for color and presentation. Now you can alternately use different ingredients in the rolls for different color and taste combinations.

When you are all done you will have bits and pieces of zucchini, yam, purple cabbage and carrots left over. Don't throw them away or compost them just yet. You can use them to make hor 'deurves and Dim Sum or finger foods. Just cut the purple cabbage into interesting shapes like triangles and cut the various pieces of vegetables and fruit you have into interesting slivers and shapes. Then assemble them together to form sculptors and interesting edible art. But a dab of different miso, pineapple, various pieces and slivers of vegetables to make really great looking Dim Sum, hour 'deuvers and finger foods. Some friends and I did this recently at the Mill Valley Film Festival and people all loved it. We were one of the most popular booths there people were telling us, I was so happy and honored when Roxanne came to our booth!

The miso already has a nice salty soy bean flavor but if you would like some dipping sauce you can combine some azuki bean miso with a little water or blend some pineapple with a little White Mellow Miso, sea salt and water. Makes a dozen or more servings. You may also try the different dressings for a dipping sauce too. There are photos on the cover.

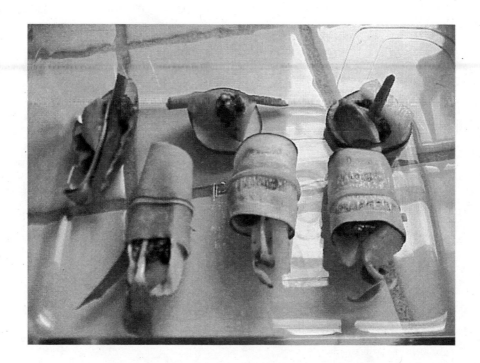

Tamale

rowing up in Los Angeles, living in the Mission in San Francisco and traveling to beautiful Mexico made me truly appreciate great Mexican food and culture! This inspired me to create an entire RAW Mexican Menu and now there is the healthiest Raw Organic Mexican Menu! This particular recipe is very versatile because you can use this "Nacho Cheese" Pine Nut Sauce in unlimited ways. It has no corn but it tastes like it does and is even creamier while also having that nacho cheese flavor too. Everyone has been raving about this new never before seen recipe and I get huge requests for it.

4 SERVINGS

4 Pieces of Kale

"Nacho Cheese" Pine Nut Sauce:
2 Cups of Pine Nuts
1 Tablespoon of Turmeric
2 Tablespoons of Hawaiian White Miso
Sea Salt
½ Lemon (optional)
¼ Cup Water
Diced Tomatoes, sliced Olives, small Pineapple chunks for garnish

"Nacho Cheese" Pine Nut Sauce: In a Blend-Tec Blender add water first, then the pine nuts, turmeric, miso, sea salt, a few drops of lemon (optional) then blend for 2 to 3 minutes for a chunkier consistency and longer for a smoother finer blend. Fill the kale pieces with this "Nacho Cheese" Pine Nut Sauce and you can use a spoon to spoon the mixture into the kale pieces. Add chucks of tomatoes, pineapple and olives and you have an instant Fiesta. Ole! The Kale looks like corn husks and the sauce is the Tamale. You can also add some guacamole and salsa on the side.

The same exact Pine Nut Sauce will be used in the Macaroni and Cheese recipe! You can also add water to it and use it as a salad dressing, a soup, a veggie dip and it will be used in the Super Nachos Recipe too.

There is a photo on the front cover.

Macaroni & Cheese

As far as I know this is the ONLY RAW Vegan Organic Macaroni & Cheese Recipe in existence! I had to come up with a fun Raw Organic version out of necessity because the cooked version used to be my favorite as a kid until I found out about all the artificial colors, chemicals and preservatives that went into it! Someday things like that will be a distant memory, that is what is so exciting about the RAW Organic Cuisine, it is so pure, healthy and decadently all natural. I brought this one to a Thanksgiving potluck and it disappeared in an instant! It is a great Holiday dish, the presentation and colors are so inviting. I hope you enjoy this special creation of mine as it is a very popular comfort food, I also wanted to bring out more new innovative never before seen Raw Organic Recipes and foods. My version looks and tastes cooked and is the creamiest.

5 Servings

2 Large Peeled Yams

"Nacho Cheese" Pine Nut Sauce:

1 ½ Cup Pine Nuts

2 Tablespoons Turmeric

¼ Cup Olive Oil

1/3 Cup Water

½ Teaspoon Sea Salt

2 Tablespoons Hawaiian Mellow White Miso for less salty flavor, 3 to 4 Tablespoons of Miso for stronger Flavor

Using a Mandolin slicer carefully make as many length wise thin slices of Yams after peeling them first. Then stack the slices of Yams on top of each other and make a sort of roll so you can carefully slice them into small thin macaroni shapes with a knife and make them curly. Do this with both Yams then put into a bowl or Pyrex glass pan. Drizzle olive oil and squeeze some lemon juice on top. Sprinkle some sea salt on top of the yams then mix the yams and make sure all the pieces are covered in olive oil then set aside to allow it to marinate.

Make the "Nacho Cheese" Sauce in a blender then pour on top of the Yams and mix again until all the pieces are covered in the "Nacho Cheese" Pine Nut Sauce. Let sit for 10 minutes so that it can absorb the sauce and soften then enjoy! The longer you let it sit the softer it gets. I am planning on packaging the "Nacho Cheese" Pine Nut Sauce to sell in all the grocery and health food stores so more people can have access to RAW Organic goodness! There is a glowing yellow photograph of this innovative new recipe in glass Pyrex ware on the cover with a pineapple, apple and some melons in the background.

Tacos

I have created a very interesting "Ground Beef", it is made from blended sunflower seeds, olive spread or tapenade that you can buy in a jar or you can blend/food process your own, some olive oil, a tiny bit of sea salt and lemon juice. Mix them together and you have greasy "Ground Beef." This will be used in the Tacos, Super Nachos, Tostada and Burritos.

4 Servings

4 Pieces of Lettuce

2 Cups of Sunflower Seeds

1 Tablespoon of Kalamata Olive Spread from a Jar or Tapenade

Olive Oil

½ Lime

Sea Salt

Diced Tomatoes

2 Tablespoons of Hawaiian Mellow White Miso

2 Large Avocados

Kelp Granules with Cayenne Pepper

Sliced Olives

Sunflower Sprouts

1 Red Bell Pepper

"Ground Beef": In the Blend-Tec Blender add the sunflower seeds and blend to a semi smooth consistency that is still chunky like around 2 minutes. You want it to be the same consistency as ground "you know what!" Then put in a bowl and add the olive spread from a jar, olive oil, sea salt and a few drops of lemon. Then mix with a fork and fluff it up, it should start to look like ground "beef". Set aside. This ground "beef" can be used to make "meat" balls for the marinara pasta recipe and can be used for hor deurves and finger foods.

Scoop out the avocados and put into a bowl, add sliced olives, some diced tomatoes, miso, a few dashes of sea salt, 2 to 3 large squeezes of lime, sprinkle some dulse and cayenne pepper then mash with a fork to make guacamole.

Seed the red bell pepper and blend in the Blend-Tec blender until it forms a thick paste, set aside and add to the tacos right before serving.

Now fill the folds of lettuce with some of the "ground beef" mixture, add the guacamole, some diced tomatoes, sliced olives, add the sunflower sprouts, drizzle some olive oil and enjoy! You can also use some of the "Nacho Cheese" Pine Nut Sauce for the cheese flavor and you can use some grated carrots or slivered yellow string beans for the cheddar cheese look. I will also sometimes use some pineapple chunks for a refreshing zesty flavor! You can also make pineapple salsa by mixing the pineapple with tomato chunks, cilantro and sea salt. You may also use chard leaves and different kinds of lettuces for the taco shell.

Burrito: use small chard leaves and wrap the above mixes in desired portions into a burrito.

These are perfect on the beach, at a picnic or Fiesta. There is a nice photo on the back cover, there are three tacos and some edible flowers on a blue cobalt plate.

ENTREES

Tostada

This recipes is basically like the Taco but you use purple cabbage "shells" instead. Get a purple cabbage, cut the stem off and carefully peel off the leaves so you get a perfect round tostada like shell. Then use the "Ground Beef" mixture from the Taco Recipe spoon first into the bottom of the purple cabbage shell, add a lot of Guacamole from the Spanish Lasagna Recipe, then diced tomatoes, sunflower sprouts, squeeze some lime and sprinkle some more "Ground Beef" and Dulse Cayenne Pepper on top and you have a colorful Fiesta waiting to happen! Great for parties, main entrée and people love this colorful creation! Save the extra purple cabbage leaves and pieces for other recipes. There is a nice picture on the cover, it is a large purple cabbage tostada shell with all the fixings and fillings.

2 TO 4 SERVINGS

There is a close up photo on the cover!

ENTREES

Super Nachos

Yup you guessed it! Please refer back to the Taco Recipe! Everyone loves Nachos, now there is a Super Raw Organic Living Version to try! Kids love the fluorescent colors of this recipe, it is very bright and festive, perfect for parties and to start off any Mexican meal.

1 LARGE SERVING

2 to 3 large Purple Cabbage Leaves

Some Pea Pods(optional)

Guacamole

Diced Tomatoes

Sliced Olives

"Nacho Cheese" Pine Nut Sauce

½ Lemon or Lime

Sea Salt

"Ground Beef" Sunflower Seed & Olive mixture, from Page 49 45

½ Yam (optional)

Cut purple cabbage leaves into triangular nacho chip shapes and you also use some pea pods, layer these on a plate, then add finely grated yams, Guacamole from the Spanish Lasagna Recipe, "Nacho Cheese" Pine Nut Sauce from the Tamale Recipe, p. 42 sliced olives, diced tomatoes, dulse granules with cayenne pepper, lemon and lime juice, sea salt, sprinkle some "ground beef" mixture and you have the World's most colorful crunchy super nachos!

There is a photograph on the cover, it is on a blue glass cobalt plate from Rainbow Grocery, the triangular chips are made of purple cabbage.

Pad Thai

his recipe demonstrates how Raw Organic Food can easily look and taste cooked! This is one of my popular recipes and people just can't seem to get enough of this one. It lasts for several days in the refrigerator if you do not put the sauce on top and it can be made a head of time. It is a good one to have on hand to share with guests or to bring with you when you are on the go.

5 Servings

2 Large Yams

2 Large Zucchini, one yellow and one green if possible

1 Cup Mung Bean Sprouts

2 Pieces of Kale

2 Purple Cabbage Leaves

Thinly Sliced Coconut Flesh made to look like noodles

Bunch of Basil & Rosemary

1 Lime juiced

Kelp Granules with Cayenne

Olive Oil

South River Azuki Bean Miso

¼ Cup Pine Nuts

Raw Organic Almond Butter

Using the mandolin make thin slices of yam and zucchini. Then using a knife carefully cut length wise into long thin "noodles". Also cut the kale and purple cabbage leaves in the same way. Add the mung beans and mix all of the above in a large bowl and set aside.

In a separate bowl mix the olive oil, dulse & cayenne pepper, juice from 1 lime all together then pour on top of the "noodles" mix. Then mix and serve with chopped: pine nuts, basil and rosemary on top. This is a very exotic colorful dish. You can add some fresh chilis to make it spicy! To make the Thai Sauce you can combine the South River Azuki Bean Miso with some water and drizzle over the top. Or you can mix Almond Butter with lime juice and agave to make a more traditional Thai sauce. The photo is on page 51 and on the website: http://www.rawinten.com.

Bok Choy Stir Fry

*W*ow, a bok choy stir fry that takes just a few seconds to make! It totally looks and tastes stir fried but is Raw Organic Living and fast to make! This is actually a Bok Choy stir fry that is in a Black Bean Sauce and is "Hong Kong Style". You will love this one.

2 TO 3 SERVINGS

3 Baby Bok Choy, you can also use large Bok Choy chopped into bite sizes
1 Tablespoon South River Azuki Bean Miso
1 Tablespoon Olive Oil
½ Lime juiced
Red Hot Chili Peppers

Wash then chop the bok choy into bite sized pieces and place in a bowl or serving dish. Mix all of the ingredients together and coat well. You will be so amazed how it looks and tastes stir fried. This is a very easy quick side dish and can be a main entrée if you make a larger batch.

"Steak"

This is a real novelty and actually looks and tastes like, well a "Steak", Raw Organic Living Cuisine is "meaty" and now more fun! People always ask me for Raw Organic Living Cuisine versions of different food items, it is one of the things that I enjoy doing and always come up with new recipes everyday. I finally came up with a "Steak" recipe much to everyone's surprise and delight. You will find this one really amusing and playfully delicious. It is another way to enjoy our favorite Tomato. Pair it up with the Mashed Potato and Gravy Recipe, some salad and sliced favorite vegetables on the side to have that "Steak" Dinner.

2 TO 3 SERVINGS

1 Large Tomato
2 Tablespoons South River Azuki Bean Miso
2 Tablespoons Olive Oil
½ Lime

Slice the tomato into ¼"-½" inch thick slices. Then cut into more square to rectangular "Steak" like shapes.

In a bowl mix the last 3 ingredients together really well. Then cover all the sides of the slices of tomato with the Azuki Bean Mixture using a spoon or fork. With the texture of the Azuki beans it really looks like a steak, the olive oil gives it the fried greasy look and taste. When you cut into it, it even has that medium "rare" look to it. But it is just another fun way to eat a tomato and when paired up with traditional favorite side dishes it is very satisfying.

But this "Steak" will help keep you young, fit and healthy! Being Raw Organic is about healing yourself and the planet. Now it gets even easier and is more fun too. You are increasing your health while freeing up precious resources and allowing for real peace on Earth.

Nut Loaf

This is a lot like the "Meat Loaf" but is now vegan and even better. I also invented a miso gravy that is just super nutritious and delicious: Living foods that is comfort food!

4 Servings

2 Cups Sunflower Seeds

3 Tablespoons Azuki Bean Miso

1 Sprig of finely chopped Rosemary

½ Lemon

¼ Cup grated Carrots

Kalamata Olive Spread

½ Cup soaked Buckwheat

2 Cups of Ground Golden Flax Seeds

Kelp Granules with Cayenne Pepper

Dash of Sea Salt

¼ Cup Water

In a Blend-Tec Blender add the golden flax seeds and blend into a fine powder, you may use a food processor also. Put into a bowl and set aside.

In a Blend-Tec Blender add water, sunflower seeds, buckwheat, miso, dulse and cayenne pepper, lemon, rosemary, sea salt and blend for 3 minutes. Mix in the golden flax seed mixture and then make a large ball. Knead until thick and then shape into a loaf. Thinly spread the olive spread around the outside and garnish with some basil.

The Gravy

2 to 3 Servings

1 Cup Water

2 Tablespoons of Azuki Bean Miso

4 Tablespoons of Ground Golden Flax Seeds

Pour the water into the Blend-Tec blender first then add the rest and blend until smooth. You will have the best Raw Organic Vegan Gravy in the world! You can add more ground golden flax seed to thicken it or more water to make it more liquid.

It will start to thicken on its own after you make it so you may want to pour a little more water and blend if it gets too thick or just enjoy the thickness. Pour on top of the Nut Loaf just before serving.

Mashed Potatoes & Gravy

*I*n this recipe we don't actually use Potato! Instead we use cauliflower and pine nuts with olive oil to create the creamiest and most decadent "mashed potato" ever! You will love this one.

2 SERVINGS

2 Cups Pine Nuts
1 Cup Cauliflower Tops
Finely chopped Rosemary
¼ Cup Olive Oil
¼ Cup Water
Dash of Sea Salt
3 Tablespoons Hawaiian Mellow White Miso

Pour the water into the Blend-Tec blender then add all of the above and blend until smooth.

The Gravy

3 SERVINGS

1 Cup Water
2 Tablespoons of Azuki Bean Miso
4 Tablespoons of Ground Golden Flax Seeds

Pour the water into the Blend-Tec blender first then add the rest and blend until smooth. Pour on top of the mashed Potatoes just before serving. Adjust the amount of ground golden flax seeds for the thickness and the water to make it more liquid.

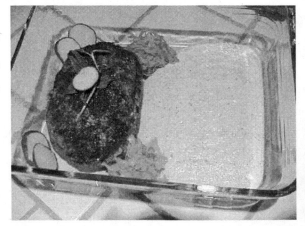

Shepherds Pie

Everyone loves Shepherds Pie! Another Raw Organic Living Comfort food that is fun and easy to make. Are you having fun or what? You should be and this pie is really fun to make because you get to use your hands to shape it.

1 TO 2 SERVINGS

You can use the Samosa Pastry Shell Recipe for a drier flakier crust or the Falafel Recipe for a moist crust for this special Shepherds Pie. Make two large balls with your hands of either of the above chosen recipes then flatten into two round circles. Carefully put one circle into a serving bowl and press down lightly, fill with the Mashed Potato and Gravy Recipe and add chopped olives, cherry tomatoes, fresh peas, grated carrots and some cubed bananas(optional) or plantain(optional). Then gently put the second circle on top of the Shepherds Pie and lovingly serve!

Sun Burger with Fries

The Sunburger is the same as the Nut Loaf but without grated carrots or olive spread. We will also make a RAW Ketchup with french fries.

Please refer to the Nut Loaf Recipe but omit the grated carrots and olive spread. You may add more ground golden flax seeds to make the burger firmer. Use your hands to roll into a ball then flatten and coat with ground golden flax seeds.

Using a mandolin cut 2 thin slices from a peeled rutabaga this will be the "bun" or you can also use 2 leaves of chard or lettuce.

2 SERVINGS

Raw Ketchup:
2 Tomatoes chopped
¼ Cup RAW Apple Cider Vinegar
¼ Cup Soaked Sundried Tomatoes
Agave to taste

Garnish:
Kosher Dill Pickles
Sunflower Sprouts
Sliced Tomatoes
1 Leaf of Lettuce
1 Large Rutabaga

To make the fries thinly cut french fry like pieces from the rutabaga. You can also sprinkle some kelp granules with cayenne pepper and drizzle with olive oil to make spicy greasy fries! Raw rutabaga has some serious super health benefits that most people are not aware of! It has more nutrients then turnips, has the most cancer fighting and anti-cancer properties out of the entire cabbage family of which it belongs to.

The Raw Ketchup: In the Blend-Tec Blender add a little water first then the tomatoes, apple cider vinegar, a dash of agave, sundried tomatoes and blend until smooth. Serve as Ketchup. To make a BBQ sauce mix some South River Azuki Bean Miso and Agave to taste.

Burger Bun: You can thinly slice 2 pieces of rutabaga, use 2 lettuce leaves or ground 1 Cup golden flax seeds and mix with a few Tablespoons water and olive oil, sprinkle a dash of sea salt then shape and compact into 2 "buns" with your hands, depending on how well you mix or compact the golden flax seed buns you might have to use a fork to eat it on a plate or the bun may stay together well enough to pick up with your hands. You can also add Raw Tahini and South River Chickpea Miso to make the Bun stay together better.

In between the buns first add a lettuce leaf, slice of tomato, the sun burger then 4 pickles and sunflower sprouts, add Raw Ketchup. Add a side of rutabaga "fries" you can also slice yellow bell peppers into thin french fry shaped "fries". Enjoy!

There is a photo on the back cover.

Sloppy Joes

Here's an All American Favorite! We are basically mixing the "Ground Beef" recipe from the Taco Recipe with Marinara Sauce to create this recipe. This one is very filling, satisfying and quick to make.

2 Servings

2 Cups of Sunflower Seeds
1 Tablespoon of Kalamata Olive Spread from a Jar or Tapenade
Olive Oil
½ Lime
Sea Salt

Marinara Sauce
2 Lettuce Leaves

Marinara Sauce:
½ Cup of Roma Tomatoes
½ Cup Sundried Tomatoes
¼ Cup Olive Oil
¼ Cup Water
Olives (optional)
Hawaiian Pineapple (optional)
Hawaiian Mellow White Miso Paste
Kelp Granules with Cayenne Pepper
Sea Salt
Finely chopped fresh Basil and Rosemary

In the Blend-Tec blender add the water, sundried tomatoes(after they have been soaked in spring water for ½ hour), 2 large tablespoons of white miso paste, olive oil, Roma tomatoes, a few dashes of the kelp granules with cayenne pepper, several pinches of sea salt, some finely chopped rosemary and basil then blend to desired consistency longer for a smooth blend and shorter for a more chunky quality.

In the Blend-Tec Blender add the sunflower seeds and blend to a semi-smooth consistency that is still chunky. You want it to be the same consistency as ground "you know what!" Then put in a bowl and add the olive spread from a jar, olive oil, sea salt and a few drops of lemon. Then mix with a fork and fluff it up, it should start to look like ground "beef". Mix with the marinara sauce in a large bowl then spoon between 2 lettuce leaves or between the Golden Flax Seed Buns from the Sunburger Recipe. The sliced olives are optional and the pineapple are optional Hawaiian twists. Simply delicious.

Chili Cheese Fries: You can even cut a lot of Yellow Bell Peppers into long french "fries" and pile them on a plate. Mix some South River Azuki Bean Miso with the Sloppy Joe mixture and pour on top of the "fries" and then drizzle some "Nacho Cheese" Pine Nut sauce from the Macaroni & Cheese Recipe and you have an instant "Chili Cheese Fries" just add some chopped tomatoes and drizzle a little olive oil on top for that greasy look and taste. Photo on hte front cover.

"Grilled Cheese" Sandwich: To make the "bread" use grind 1 Cup of Golden Flax seeds in the Blend-Tec Blender and grind into a fine powder then mix in a bowl with 2 Tablespoons of Tahini and some sea salt, mix very well then use a fork to form a flat square on a plate, cut diagonal with a knife and separate the two halves. One one half spread some "Nacho Cheese" Pine Nut Sauce from page 42. Then using a spatula carefully flip the other half on top to form a triangular "Grilled Cheese" Sandwich and enjoy!

Island Kebobs

*T*his is the most colorful vibrant festive easy picnic, beach or party entrée. I like to serve it with the Raw Macaroni and Cheese and a sun iced tea with Agave. It does require getting some bamboo skewers but if you can't find any you can also substitute them with some small smooth chopsticks.

2 Servings

2 Bamboo Skewers or 2 small smooth chopsticks

2 Zucchini

1 Red or Yellow Bell Pepper

1 Large Plantain

Some mixed Cherry Tomatoes

Pineapple from Hawaii

2 Radishes (optional)

2 Asian Pears

1 Cup Orange Juice or Pineapple Juice or Apple Juice

2 Tablespoons Agave

2 Tablespoons of Hawaiian White Mellow Miso or South River Azuki Bean Miso for a more BBQ flavor

Cut the zucchini into round medium to thick wheel slices, seed the bell pepper and cut into squares, slice the plantains into medium round wheels, wash the cherry tomatoes, chop the pineapples into medium square cubes along with the Asian Pears then start to place on the skewers or chopsticks starting with the square bell pepper then alternate with zucchini, plantain, radish, cherry tomatoes and so on. Some people will even use sliced dill kosher pickles and other fun picnic ingredients.

"Grill" Marinade Sauce: In the Blend-Tec blender, blend: the orange juice, agave and miso then dip the skewered kebobs into them to let marinate for 10 minutes or longer, the longer you allow it to marinate the softer and more "cooked" it will look and taste. Use the Cold Mountain brand Hawaiian Mellow White Miso for a more tropical and citrus taste or use the South River brand Azuki Bean Miso for a tropical BBQ Sauce. You can also use these sauces for other recipes. This is a very colorful and festive treat that is quick and easy to make. You will be amazed at how "grilled" it seems after marinating them. You can continue to drizzle more sauce while eating or use the sauce to dip while eating too. Now there are living sauces!

This recipe is especially good if you happen to have a lot of left over bits and pieces of fruit and veggies from making other Raw Recipes. There is a very colorful photograph on the cover and it is with a side of RAW Macaroni and Cheese and special raw living purple cabbage sauerkraut made by a loving couple in Berkeley near San Francisco, there contact information is:

Cultured
Po Box 2717
Berkeley, CA 947102

They did not include a Website on any of their packages I wish they did because they are so good and reasonably priced too. I really love their Sauerkraut Kim Chee the best you can add this to many different dishes to compliment them with more living energy. The Kim Chee goes really well with the California Roll for example or next to the Pad Thai too. They state on their label:

"Why Raw Sauerkraut? It's alive! Billions of beneficial microorganisms (including lactobacillus acidophilus) combine forces to restore and maintain a vibrant ecosystem of intestinal flora. When enjoyed on a regular basis, this probiotic, naturally fermented sauerkraut will energize the digestive system to increase nutrient absorption and eliminate toxins, resulting in overall superior immune system function. Restore. Revitalize."

"WOW" and I thought it just tasted really good. So many benefits, is in a nice glass jar, wonderful job you super heroes over there in Berkeley!

Samosa

*T*his Samosa looks and tastes like it is deep fried but it is completely Raw Organic and an amazing super food. You do not need to dehydrate it or anything and can enjoy it right after preparing it. At the printing of this book no one else has this recipe. Golden Flax Seeds are usually hard to digest but in this recipe we ground them into a fine powder so you are getting a lot of super flavorful nutrition and it is so simple to make.

2 SERVINGS

Samosa "Pastry":
2 Cups Golden Flax Seeds
¼ Cup Water
2 Tablespoons Olive Oil
Sea Salt to taste

Filling:
1 Asian Pear chopped into small cubes
2 Figs chopped into slices
Cherry Tomatoes chopped in half
Kosher Dill Pickle Slices
Fresh Peas

First pour the Golden Flax Seeds into the Blend-Tec Blender and blend into a smooth fine powder, you can also use a food processor. Then pour into a medium bowl. Add the water and sea salt then mix with a fork so the whole mixture becomes like a paste and is evenly moistened. Then using your hands pat down the mixture into the bottom of the bowl. Then add the filling ingredients into half side of the bowl because you will fold the other half over it to form a half moon or half circle shaped Samosa! I like to place some of the ingredients near the outer edge so when you fold it some will show on the edge and you can see the filling, it gives it a very artistic and appetizing presentation. In this recipe the Asian Pear substitutes the potatoes and the figs gives it a nice sweet flavor as well as color. You can also use or add plantain or bananas, turmeric or curry powder etc. and create your own delicious fillings.

Calzone

This is exactly like the Samosa but with a marinara, olive and nut cheese filling. I also love calzones and this one is sure to please. You can also add some pineapple chunks to give it a Hawaiian flavor. You can also warm it up in the sun and get extra natural energy. Some people like to place a glass bowl over the top of a plate and place in the sun or in a sunny window.

Calzone "Pastry":

2 Cups Golden Flax Seeds

¼ Cup Water

2 Tablespoons Olive Oil

Sea Salt to taste

First pour the Golden Flax Seeds into the Blend-Tec Blender and blend into a smooth fine powder, you can also use a food processor. Then pour into a medium bowl. Add the water and sea salt then mix with a fork so the whole mixture becomes like a paste and is evenly moistened. Then using your hands pat down the mixture into the bottom of the bowl. Then add the filling ingredients into half side of the bowl because you will fold the other half over it to form a half moon or half circle shaped Calzone.

Filling:

Marinara Sauce:

½ Cup of Roma Tomatoes

½ Cup Sundried Tomatoes

¼ Cup Olive Oil

Olives

Hawaiian Pineapple from Maui

Hawaiian Mellow White Miso Paste

Kelp Granules with Cayenne Pepper

Sea Salt

Some finely chopped Basil and Rosemary

Nut Cheese:

1 Cup Brazil Nuts or Pine Nuts

¼ Cup Water

¼ Cup Olive Oil

2 Tablespoons Miso

Sea Salt

In the Blend-Tec blender, blend the sundried tomatoes(after they have been soaked in spring water for ½ hour), 2 large tablespoons of white miso paste, olive oil, Roma tomatoes, a few dashes of the Kelp Granules with Cayenne Pepper. Several pinches of sea salt, several sprigs of chopped Rosemary and Basil then blend to desired consistency longer for a smooth blend and shorter for a more chunky quality.

For the nut cheese, blend all the ingredients in the Blend-Tec Blender. You can also use the "Nacho Cheese" Pine Nut Sauce from the Macaroni and Cheese recipe instead.

Pour the Marinara Sauce and some Nut Cheese over half the Calzone mixture, add sliced olives and pineapple(optional) and fold over to form a half circle Calzone.

"Chicken" and "Turkey"

Part of the fun of being vegetarian and vegan is seeing what you can make that will taste like well "you know what!" It has been said many times so I don't want to repeat the "it tastes like..." you know what! I created a very quick, easy and fun way to make a "Chicken" or "Turkey" that you can use for main entrees and for the holidays.

4 SERVINGS

2 to 3 Fresh Young Coconuts Meat carefully scraped

2 Tablespoons Olive Oil

¼ Cup Turmeric

¼ Cup Curry Powder (optional)

Kelp Granules with Cayenne Pepper (optional)

Chopped Pine Nuts (optional)

Ground Gold Flax Seeds (optional)

Sea Salt to taste

There are different techniques for scraping coconut meat. Some people like to use a spoon and others even use a rubber spatula to carefully get the creamy flesh. Whichever method you use please be extra careful to go over the coconut meat again to make sure you do not have any splinters or shell pieces still attached to he meat. These are too hard to chew and don't digest well so make sure to go over the meat that you got from the coconut 2 to 3 times, you can just as easily scrape all of it with a spoon to make doubly sure.

There are also in general 2 types of coconut flesh that you will encounter, a thin very soft almost translucent one and a very thick hard one, if it is purple than it is over ripe and bad and should be composted. For this recipe you only want to use the thinner soft almost translucent coconut flesh. The thicker harder coconut flesh is best for desserts and smoothies and can be stored in a glass container in the refrigerator.

In a bowl or shallow pan place the coconut flesh down and sprinkle the turmeric, curry powder, sea salt, dulse & cayenne and olive oil over it and you can sprinkle a little more turmeric and curry powder after coating it with olive oil. You can also mix it to make sure all the pieces are covered, let sit for 10 minutes or longer and serve. The longer you let it marinate the more flavor it will absorb and the softer it will become. You can serve this with a side of salad, macaroni and cheese, mashed potatoes for a down home comfort meal. For a "fried" or "baked" "chicken" you can coat it with finely chopped pine nuts for that extra crunchy flavor or use the fine golden flax seed powder to give it that "fried bread crumb" texture.

To make the "Turkey" you can marinate the coconut flesh in a mixture of: 1 cup of orange juice, 2 Tablespoons of Miso and 2 tablespoons of Agave first then follow the "chicken " recipe. Feel free to experiment with the different amounts of turmeric, curry powder, etc. You can add more spice and call it a Jamaican Jerk "Chicken" or Thai "Chicken" and you can use it in the Kebob Skewers Recipe too.

Holiday Stuffing

This is a great Holiday Stuffing! Perfect for Thanksgiving or Christmas and other holidays. Now you can really give thanks to nature and all her splendor. It is a delicious medley of fruit and veggies. A really Raw Living Organic Special treat!

8 SERVINGS

2 Asian Pears

1 Mango peeled

1 Large Cucumber peeled

Ground Golden Flax Seeds

Soaked Sunflower Seeds

Soaked Chickpeas

Chopped Butternut or Spaghetti Squash

Finely Chopped Basil and Rosemary

Finely Grated Yams (optional)

Large Grated Zucchini

Cherry Tomatoes halved

Chopped Pine Nuts

5 Tablespoons of Olive Oil

3 Tablespoons of South River Azuki Bean Miso

2 Tablespoons of South River Chickpea Miso

Kelp Granules with Cayenne Pepper

Sea Salt to taste

Pomegranate

Chopped Walnuts

Chop the first three ingredients into small cubes then mix the rest of the ingredients in a large bowl and serve. Now that you are eating living foods you are truly connecting with the special forces and miracles in the universe.

Variations: Shape the Falafel Recipe into small cubes and add some "Ground Beef" from the Taco Recipe.

The pomegranate adds a nice Holiday twist and festive color. Raw Organic Living Cuisine always creates a cause to celebrate. I have been to so many special Holiday Raw Organic parties, events and potlucks. They are all very warm, loving, super creative and are just the best ever. May you and yours enjoy all the blessings and gifts in life.

Falafels

A Falafel Recipe that does not require dehydrating and can be made very quickly. One of my favorites and a good one to keep on hand in the refrigerator for parties or guests. It looks and tastes deep fried! And can be made in an instant.

8 SERVINGS

1 Cup ground Golden Flax Seeds

1 Tablespoon Raw Organic Tahini

3 to 4 Tablespoons South River Chickpea Miso

½ Cup soaked Chickpeas (optional)

Chopped Rosemary and Basil

5 Tablespoons Olive Oil

2 Tablespoons Water

Sea Salt to taste

Kelp Granules with Cayenne Pepper

Finely Chopped Basil and Rosemary

Pine Nut "Yogurt" Sauce:

1 Cup Pine Nuts

¼ Cup Water

2 Tablespoons Miso

3 Tablespoons Olive Oil

Finely Chopped Dill (optional) and Rosemary

Kelp Granules with Cayenne Pepper

Sea Salt

Lemon Juice to taste (optional)

Blend the soaked chickpeas (optional and can be omitted to save time when using the South River Chickpea Miso) in the Blend-Tec Blender or a food processor then mix with all the other ingredients in a large bowl then form falafel balls with your hands and serve with Pine Nut sauce, sunflower sprouts, chopped tomatoes and cucumber wrapped in red lettuce or chard leaves!

Variations: You can form a burger shape with this and call it a "chicken pattie" or make "nugget" shapes and serve with Barbecue Sauce! Your kids will love these Raw Nuggets and it should only take a few minutes to make! They can even help you make the shapes. For BBQ Sauce go to the Sunburger Recipe and make the Raw Ketchup then blend with some South River Azuki Bean Miso and Agave to taste.

Oatmeal and Cereal

This is a favorite Breakfast Entree and snack. We will be using the Almond Pulp and Almond Milk from this recipe in many other recipes and desserts.

2 SERVINGS

Oatmeal and Cereal:

2 Cups of Golden Flax Seeds

Almond Milk:

3 Cups of soaked Almonds

4 Cups Water

¼ Cup of Agave

Cinnamon (optional)

Almond Milk: First pour the water into the Blend-Tec blender then the soaked Almonds with ¼ cup of Agave to sweeten and blend until the almonds become very small crumbs in size. Then strain into a large bowl using a cheese cloth and make almond milk, save the almond pulp to make RAW cookies, pie shells, desserts and more! Set aside the almond milk, you can use the almond milk for smoothies, the Chocolate Shake Recipe and more.

Oatmeal and Cereal: Put into the blender 2 cups of flax seeds and blend until it becomes a fine powder about 5 minutes. You can also use a food processor.

Put the golden flax seed powder into a bowl and then add the almond milk on top and slightly stir. It looks and tastes just like a "cooked" Oatmeal or breakfast cereal but is totally vegan, organic and RAW! The Golden Flax has an incredible energy with healing properties, the oil in it has amazing power that is usually very expensive in the health food store. Now you are getting all the benefits and when you ground flax seeds it is easier for the body to digest. The Almond Milk has great enzymes and nutrition as well. This is a very quick and easy Raw Breakfast treat! Raw Breakfast recipes that look and taste like the "cooked" version are rare and not easy to come by, I came up with this one while at the Tree Of Life Rejuvenation Center. You can use the left over Almond Pulp to make amazing desserts, cookies and pie shell crusts which I will show you how in later recipes and chapters. You can also add your favorite fruit on top like blueberries, strawberries, soaked Tibetan Goji Berries or cinnamon. Yum!

SOUPS

Creamy Tomato

Spicy Avocado

Carrot Ginger

"Clam" Chowder

Thai Coconut Soup

Creamy Tomato Soup

*T*his is one of the most creamy and rejuvenating soups on the planet. All of these soups are very easy to prepare and only take a few minutes. I have found that adding sunflower sprouts on top of any soup gives it a sort of "noodle" and it tastes great while being a great complimentary garnish too. You can also add chopped baby spinach, slices of avocado or red bell peppers for garnish. This creamy tomato soup is very popular.

2 SERVINGS

4 Roma or 2 regular Tomatoes

4 to 5 Pieces of Soaked Sundried Tomatoes for ½ hour in water

3 Tablespoons of Hawaiian White Mellow Miso

¼ Cup Olive Oil

3 Cups Water

Finely Chopped Basil and Rosemary to taste

Kelp Granules with Cayenne Pepper (optional)

Sea Salt to taste

Place all the ingredients in the Blend-Tec Blender and blend until smooth. You may serve with extra dulse granules and cayenne, olive oil and your choice of garnishes.

Spicy Avocado Soup

This soup is nice and spicy and it can be used as a salad dressing as well. To make it a salad dressing you can add a little more olive oil and a few teaspoons of Agave to taste.

2 SERVINGS

2 Avocados

4 Tablespoons of Hawaiian White Mellow Miso

¼ Cup Olive Oil

3 Cups Water

1 Lime juiced

Finely Chopped Basil, Cilantro and Rosemary to tasteKelp & Cayenne pepper to taste

½ Hot Chili Pepper

Sea Salt to taste

Place all the ingredients in the Blend-Tec Blender and blend until smooth. This soup has such a great creamy spicy flavor, perfect for winter or chilly days. For extra color and flavor you can add grated carrots and pieces of purple cabbage before blending.

Variation: To make a spicy Broccoli Soup you can add a few broccoli tops as well right before blending.

Carrot Ginger Soup

I *like the color and spice of this soup. It is great on cold or chilly days to warm up your spirit.*

2 Servings

2 Large Grated Carrots

1 Tablespoon grated or chopped ginger

3 Tablespoons of Hawaiian White Mellow Miso

¼ Cup Olive Oil

3 Cups Water

Finely Chopped Rosemary to taste

Kelp Granules with Cayenne Pepper to taste

Red Hot Chili Peppers (optional for extra spice! One of my favorite bands in the World, I had a special Raw Living Food Dinner with them once in Hollywood! Anthony and Flea you rock!)

Sea Salt to taste

Pour the water first then place all the ingredients in the Blend-Tec Blender and blend until smooth. For extra color and flavor you can add grated zucchini and pieces of purple cabbage before blending.

"Clam" Chowder

This will look and taste so much like "Clam" Chowder that it will amaze you. A Bay Area specialty and favorite now with a Raw Organic Version.

2 SERVINGS

1 ½ Cup Cauliflower tops

4 Brazil Nuts

½ Lemon juiced

1 Teaspoon grated or chopped Ginger

4 Tablespoons of Hawaiian White Mellow Miso

¼ Cup Olive Oil

3 Cups Water

Finely Chopped Basil and Rosemary to taste

1 Teaspoon Kelp Granules with Cayenne

Sliced Kalamata olives that are sliced into small wheels then sliced again in half

Small Pineapple chunks

Sea Salt to taste

Place all the ingredients in the Blend-Tec Blender except for the olives and pineapples and blend until smooth. Add the sliced olives and pineapple and serve.

Thai Coconut Soup

I love Thai Cuisine for its spicy colorful exotic flavors. Thai cuisine is gaining popularity around the world for its spicy, vibrant taste. I've been getting a lot of requests for this specially guarded secret recipe, so here it is!

2 SERVINGS

1 Fresh Young Coconut with the water and carefully scraped coconut flesh

Some grated carrots, zucchini and small pieces of purple cabbage

1 Lime juiced

1 Teaspoon grated or chopped Ginger

3 to 4 Tablespoons of Hawaiian White Mellow Miso

¼ Cup Olive Oil

3 Cups Water

Finely Chopped Basil, Cilantro and Rosemary to taste

Kelp Granules with Cayenne to taste

Sea Salt to taste

½ Hot Chili Pepper for extra spicy flavor (optional)

Small Pineapple chunks

Pour the water into the Blend-Tec blender first then add all the ingredients except for the pineapples and blend until smooth. Add the pineapple and serve.

DRESSINGS

Surfs Up Dressing

Orange Delight Dressing

Sweet Mustard Dressing

Ranch Dressing

Red Lava Dressing

Island Mango Dressing

Hawaiian Pineapple Dressing

Surfs Up Dressing

All of my dressings are quick and easy of course. I grew up in Los Angeles so Surfing was a big part of my life and I love Surfing in Hawaii. I also enjoy Island and Surfing inspired recipes because they are always delicious, youthful, rejuvenating and refreshing. This Surfs Up Dressing is so named because of the sea vegetables you can use and the kelp that is in the recipe. It's quick, delicious, very different and you will be getting plenty of minerals that your body needs and loves! There are a few different ways to make this dressing.

3 Servings

1 Cup Olive Oil
½ Cup Soaked Sunflower Seeds
¼ Teaspoon of powdered Kelp or other Sea Vegetable
½ Teaspoon Vita Mineral Green Powder (optional)
½ Lemon
Agave to desired taste

Put all the ingredients in the Blend-Tec Blender and make waves by blending to desired consistency.

Variations: You can also add some horseradish or mustard to make it spicy, you can add some fresh grated ginger, or even just some avocado instead of the soaked sunflower seeds. Some fresh Rosemary or Basil is great too, add your favorite fresh herb. The above recipe is the quick basic, you can always make it even better and just the way you like it. Just ride the wave!

Health Force Nutritionals brand makes the most amazing Raw Green Powder that has like very thing that is good under the sun in it! Their ingredients list is long and is just the best on the market for a very good price. I have met the regional sales director at sample booths and demonstrations and they are super nice with the best all natural products, the Vita Mineral Green Powder is the ultimate green powder! Their Website: Healthforce.com. We will be using it in the Green Power Smoothie. You can always sprinkle a little on top of soups and salads for extra super energy and power.

I would put this dressing on top of Organic Baby Asian Salad Mix that you can buy at Trader Joe's. I would add some sunflower sprouts, sundried dulse, Raw Kim Chee or Raw Sauerkraut from the jar and maybe even some figs for color and sweetness or fresh pineapple then toss the dressing on top and you are Surfing it up in your living salad!

Orange Delight Dressing

When I was in The Bahamas I liked to use this quick simple but totally delicious dressing. It is a really good one when you don't have much time and a lot of guests to serve. Although simple the flavor is really nice and refreshing.

4 SERVINGS

2 Oranges juiced
1 Cup Olive Oil
1 Tablespoon Miso (optional)

Just mix the above in a bowl or Blend-Tec blender and serve over salad or veggies. You can also blend with ½ Cup of soaked sunflower seeds, pine nuts or soaked Almonds for a creamier dressing or dip. But it is just as refreshing with just juice and olive oil and a bit of Miso. Pour over your favorite light salad or just some sprouts.

Sweet Mustard Dressing

*E*veryone loves the sweet and sour taste of sweet mustard dressings. Well this one is low glycemic with less sugar and the ultimate in health. Tangy and tasty!

4 SERVINGS

½ Cup Olive Oil

¼ Cup Water

1 Teaspoon dry Mustard or Horseradish

A few pieces of Purple Cabbage (optional)

1 Tablespoon Miso

3 Tablespoons Agave

5 Soaked Almonds or ¼ Cup Pine Nuts

¼ Cup Raw Apple Cider Vinegar

Sea Salt to taste

Put all the ingredients into the Blend-Tec Blender and blend until smooth. It has a nice sweet and sour taste that goes well over a cucumber or green papaya salad.

not great too bland

Ranch Dressing

Just think, a Heavenly Raw Organic Vegan Ranch Dressing that is super creamy and decadent. Enjoy!

4 SERVINGS

1 Cup Water

1 Cup Soaked Almonds

Finely chopped Rosemary and Basil

Some grated Carrots, small chopped Red & Yellow Bell Peppers

Some Cucumbers and pieces of Purple Cabbage

1 Teaspoon of Agave

2 Tablespoons of Lemon juice

Sea Salt to taste

Blend the almonds and water in the Blend-Tec Blender until very smooth. Place in a bowl and mix in all the rest of the seasonings and lemon juice. It is so creamy on salads and sprout salads.

Ranch is one of my personal favorite dressings.

Red Lava Dressing

A nice red lava like spread and dressing. Hawaii inspired this recipe as it still has live lava flows that are creating new parts of the Island. Something about the bright red color of lava and red bell peppers is very attractive and magical.

2 TO 3 SERVINGS

1 Red Bell Pepper

1 Cup soaked Almonds, or Pine Nuts or Brazil Nuts

1 Tablespoon Hawaiian Mellow White Miso

1/4 Cup Lemon Juice

Some fresh chopped Basil and Rosemary

1 Tablespoon of Agave

Sea Salt to taste

Seed the Red Bell Pepper and blend all the rest in the Blend-Tec blender until super smooth. It will thicken after and you can use it as a spread in lettuce wraps, tacos, enchiladas, tostadas, etc. To make into a salad dressing just add another ½ Cup of water, 2 tablespoons of Miso and ½ Cup of olive oil. I love the red lava like color of this recipe. You can also add some Hawaiian pineapple chunks before blending for a real Luau flavor.

Island Mango Dressing

Hawaii has a very special place in my heart because of all the fantastic adventures and friends that I have there. It literally is a fantasy Island in many ways. Now we can share in the fantasy with this dressing.

2 TO 3 SERVINGS

1 Ripe Mango

1 Tablespoon finely chopped Ginger

¼ Cup Water

Olive Oil to taste

1 Tablespoon of Hawaiian Mellow White Miso

1 Tablespoon Agave

Pour the water in first then blend all of the above in a Blend-Tec Blender until smooth. You may substitute the water with fresh apple juice. Nice sweet Island Mango Dressing to remind you of PA-RAW-DISE! Yes Heaven does exist on Earth and you can make it happen in your dressings and salad! Organic food is such a blessing because if you enjoy it in the right ways then more miracles will manifest on many levels. I have seen this happen for a lot of people and in my own life. Now with this dressing Hawaii and PA-RAW-DISE does not seem so far away.

Hawaiian Pineapple Dressing

I love Hawaii and anything Hawaiian! A pure Paradise Tropical Island in the middle of the Pacific Ocean with perfect: weather, surf, fruits and vegetables all year around. And now a huge growing Raw Organic Population too.

2 TO 3 SERVINGS

¼ Cup Water

½ Cup Pineapple chunks

1 Tablespoon of Hawaiian Mellow White Miso

1 Tablespoon Agave

Sea Salt to taste

Turmeric to taste (optional)

First pour the water into the Blend-Tec Blender then throw all the rest of the ingredients into the Blend–Tec Blender and blend until smooth. The Turmeric will add a spicy intense yellow color and taste! A Tropical Parawdise in your kitchen. Definitely a good dressing over a cucumber salad, mango salad or your favorite green salad.

DESSERTS

Mango Cheesecake

Strawberry Cream Pie

Banana Cream Pie

Coconut Cream Pie

Carrot Cake

Triple Layer Chocolate Cake

RAWos

RAWinkies

Pancakes

Crepes

RAWsmores

Baklava

Chocolate Chip Cookies

Ginger Cookies

Energy Bars

Tibetan Goji Berry Macaroons

Mango & Coconut Cream

Blueberry Mousse

DESSERTS

Mango Cheesecake

This is such an amazing crowd pleaser and colorful vibrant dessert that everyone will love. The bright yellow vegan version will cheer up all "cheesecake" lovers!

2 TO 3 SERVINGS

1 Large Mango

1 ½ Cups of Brazil Nuts

¼ Cup Agave

½ Cup Water

Soaked Almond Pulp from Almond Milk Recipe in the RAW Oatmeal and Cereal Recipe mixed with ¼ cup Agave(we will be using this a lot for all of the desserts!), Page 71

In the Blend-Tec blender add the water first, then Brazil nuts, chopped mango and agave and blend until smooth.

Almond Pie Crust: In a glass round pan cover the bottom with the almond pulp that is already mixed with the ¼ cup agave, press down to make it a crust.

Then pour the Mango Cheesecake mix over the crust and serve right away or let chill for 1 hour It is so colorful and delicious! Brazil nuts only grow in the Rainforest and has great healing powers, enzymes and vitamins. You can garnish with sliced strawberries or soaked Tibetan Goji Berries for a colorful dramatic gourmet presentation. This is a real super creamy healthy dessert and there is a nice photo on the cover.

Strawberry Cream Pie

Strawberry is one of my favorite fruits, this recipe is sure to delight strawberry fans. It's naturally sweet and organic bliss.

2 TO 3 SERVINGS

2 Cups Strawberry

1 ½ Cups of Brazil Nuts or soaked Almonds or soaked Sunflower Seeds or Pine Nuts

¼ Cup Agave

½ Cup Water

Left over Soaked Almond Pulp from Almond Milk mixed with ¼ cup Agave, Page 71

1 ½ Cups Pistachio Nuts

1/4 Cup soaked Tibetan Goji Berries(optional)

This recipe can be made in many quick easy ways and I will go though them with you. You can use the nuts to make a really decadent creamy strawberry cream pie or if you don't have much time you can just mash several bananas with the strawberries and agave for a quick dessert. The almond pulp and agave is a more traditional looking crust. But for the most dramatic gourmet creation I recommend using the Pistachio Nuts blended with some coconut meat(optional) and agave, you may also use a food processor and the coconut meat will keep the crust together while making it creamier. In a glass round pan cover the bottom with the almond pulp that is already mixed with the agave or pistachio nut mixture and press down to make it a crust.

In the Blend-Tec Blender put the water in first, then the strawberries, your choice of nuts, agave and blend until smooth. Then pour the Strawberry Cream mix over the crust and serve right away or let chill for 1 in the refrigerator. To make this strawberry cream pie even more amazing you can add the soaked Tibetan Goji Berries right before blending the strawberry mixture to make this pie a super food! You can also use some extra soaked Tibetan Goji Berries as a garnish along with sliced strawberries. To make the pie thicker add a few more nuts at a time. I love how the bright green color of the pistachios contrasts with the pink color of the strawberries. This is a very gourmet super dessert.

Banana Cream Pie

I found that kids really love this recipe. Their parents always requested extra for themselves and for their children. I am more than happy to share this recipe with you and your family.

2 TO 3 SERVINGS

1 Banana
1 ½ Cups soaked Sunflower seeds or soaked Almonds or soaked Pine Nuts
¼ Cup Agave
¼ Cup Water
Left over Soaked Almond Pulp from Almond Milk mixed with ¼ cup Agave, Page 71
Soaked Tibetan Goji Berries and sliced Banana for garnish
Cinnamon to taste

This super creamy Banana Cream Pie doesn't even need a crust but if you would like to use one then I would recommend using the Almond Pulp Agave mixture. You can also add some carob powder to taste to make a "chocolate crust". Press into a single round glass serving bowl, to make a whole pie triple this recipe accordingly.

In the Blend-Tec Blender put the water in first, bananas, agave, a few sprinkles of cinnamon, your choice of nuts but I suggest using the soaked sunflower seeds for this one. I am suggesting different nuts so you can try different flavors and combinations but have found the sunflower seeds to be the best one for this recipe. Blend until smooth. Then pour the Banana Cream mixture over the crust and serve right away or let chill in the refrigerator for 10-30 minutes. Garnish with soaked Tibetan Goji Berries and slices of banana and sprinkle some cinnamon on top. Kids really love this one and I get plenty of requests for it all the time. If you squeeze some lemon on top it will the color from getting really dark on top. I just wanted to let you know that the color will change very quickly and will get browner even if you put in the refrigerator. So try to serve this after making or soon after. You can also scrape off the thin top layer before serving if you are storing it. Photo on back cover.

Coconut Cream Pie

This super creamy Coconut Pie reminds me of the sun and fresh ocean breezes of the Islands. It is so refreshingly creamy and smooth.

2 TO 3 SERVINGS

2 to 3 Fresh Young Coconuts with the meat carefully scraped out of the shells

3 Tablespoons of Nutiva Raw Extra Virgin Coconut Oil

1/4 Cup Agave

1/4 Cup Water

Soaked Almond Pulp from Almond Milk Recipe mixed with ¼ Cup Agave, Page 71

Cinnamon to taste

Carob Powder to taste (optional)

First press the Almond Pulp Agave mixture into a round glass pan with a spoon.

In the Blend-Tec Blender pour the water first, then coconut meat, coconut oil, agave, dash of cinnamon and blend until smooth. Pour over the crust and serve or allow to chill in the fridge until firm, sprinkle with a little cinnamon before serving. For an interesting twist you can also add some soaked Tibetan Goji Berries before blending or mix the almond pulp and agave with carob powder to make a "chocolate" crust. You will love this and want to make more all the time! The fresh coconut and coconut oil have so many all natural anti-aging properties and health benefits, finally decadent amazing desserts that are actually really good for you! Since none of the crusts are dehydrated it will be moist, so press down hard to make it more compact, it is a living crust! There is a photo on the back cover with a carob powder "chocolate" crust with some pineapple and melons in the background.

Carrot Cake

I'*s carrot and cake. A favorite combination and now Raw Organic and Living The unbaked Carrot Cake dessert!*

Filling:

2 Large grated Carrots

2 Cups Soaked Almond Pulp from Almond Milk in the Oatmeal and Cereal Recipe mixed with ¼ Cup Agave, Page 71

½ Cup Coconut Flesh

¼ Cup Agave

½ Cup Water

Cinnamon to taste

Frosting:

1 Cup Pine Nuts

2 to 3 Tablespoons of Nutiva Coconut Oil

¼ Cup Water

3 Tablespoons Agave

Cinnamon to taste

Crust:

Soaked Almond Pulp from Almond Milk mixed with ¼ Cup Agave, Page 71

In the blender add water, grated carrots, coconut, cinnamon and agave and blend until smooth. Then pour into a bowl that has 2 cups of almond pulp and lightly mix and fluff up with a fork.

In a glass round pan cover the bottom with the almond pulp that is already mixed with the ¼ cup agave, press down to make it a crust. Then spoon the Carrot Cake mix over the crust and serve right away or let chill in the refrigerator. You can also add carob powder to the crust and mix to make a "chocolate" crust.

To make the Frosting pour the water in the Blend-Tec Blender first then put in all the rest of the ingredients and blend until smooth then pour over the Carrot Cake and serve.

Variation: Blend 2 Cups Pistachio Nuts or Pecans with some coconut meat, agave and press into a glass pan for the crust.

Triple Layer Chocolate Cake

This one is for all of you chocolate lovers out there! What else is dessert for? Chocolate of course! Well we use Raw Organic Carob Powder in this healthy decadent creamy recipe for your enjoyment and super health. It looks and tastes just like chocolate but with super all natural health benefits.

3 TO 4 SERVINGS

1 **Fresh Young Coconut with the meat carefully scraped out**

1 **Tablespoon of Nutiva Extra Virgin Coconut Oil**

4 **Tablespoons Agave**

¼ **Cup Water**

½ **Cup Pine Nuts**

Soaked Almond Pulp from Almond Milk Recipe mixed with ¼ Cup Agave, Page 71

Cinnamon

Carob Powder to taste

This will be the quickest triple layer chocolate cake you will ever make. And the best one too because most of it will be living and will connect you with true health and beauty. It will be the most decadent taste and scrumptious cake you ever tasted. You save so much time by not having to bake it. You may also add blackberries and raspberries in between the layers or strawberries to make a black forest type of dessert cake.

Mix the Carob Powder with the Almond Pulp to desired level of chocolateness then mix in the Agave and press with a spoon into several round glass serving containers.

In the Blend-Tec Blender put in the water, pine nuts, agave, carob powder to taste, about 2 to 3 tablespoons is the suggested amount. Pour over the almond pulp to form the 2nd layer.

In the Blend-Tec Blender put the water, coconut meat, coconut oil, agave, carob powder and blend until smooth. Pour over the 2nd layer to form the 3rd layer and serve or allow to chill in the fridge until firm, sprinkle with a little cinnamon before serving. For a more gourmet presentation you can make round cookie cutter shapes our of paper and tape. Gourmet Chefs will use a bio degradable corn plastic that is see through and tape to make a tubular shape. Place in the middle of a plate and fill with the 3 different layers, you may add your favorite berries in between the layers and on top as well. Then allow to chill and harden in the fridge and then cut the tape or carefully remove the taped paper or bio degradable corn plastic and serve.

Some variations on this recipe is to use different layers like one carob almond pulp layer with a mango cheesecake layer combination or even with the strawberry cream pie mixture, use your imagination and creativity. The photo is at the bottom of this page and on the website.

Tiramisu: To make the Tiramisu form 3 long cookies with the Almond Pulp Agave mixture. Then spoon the first layer from the Triple Chocolate Cake recipe around the cookies and pat down with a spoon or your hands to make it firm. Then pour the second layer from the Triple Layer Chocolate Cake recipe over everything, then you can make a coconut cream with some coconut and agave or make a pine nut cream or almond cream by blending with some water and agave to taste. Sprinkle some cinnamon on top and you have Tiramisu! It is very similar to the Triple Layer Chocolate Cake but with the plain Almond Pulp Agave cookies and a "whipped cream" on top with cinnamon. You can also use bananas to make the cookies. There is a photo on the back cover.

DESSERTS

Raweo

*T*his version has no transfat or artificial anything. We are all natural organic beings and it makes no sense to be putting things in or on our bodies that are not all natural and organic! More people are waking up to this fact and I am more than pleased and honored to help make it a truly enjoyable gourmet sweet experience. I know you will love this easy delectable childhood favorite treat! People tell me they can't get enough of Raweos and love it a lot. Kids really go all out for this recipe, the love to make and eat them. Parents like it because they know it is low glycemic and sugar so is very well balanced. This RAWeo is actually a living food because the nuts are soaked so you are getting even more nutritious goodness in each bite! A dessert that is actually good for you on many levels. This one also travels well.

8 Servings

2 Cups soaked Almonds, you can also use and substitute 2 Cups soaked Sunflower Seeds if you cannot find or have access to Raw Organic Almonds

2 Cups Water

5 Tablespoons Carob Powder

5 Tablespoons Agave

Nutiva Raw Extra Virgin Coconut Oil

Cheesecloth

Small Cookie Cutters

Put the Almonds and Water into the Blend-Tec Blender and blend until the almonds become very small crumb like in size. Pour into Cheesecloth over a large mixing bowl. Squeeze all the almond milk you can out of the almond pulp and save the pulp. Later you can experiment and make them as moist or dry as you like. Save the almond milk to drink straight, you can add some agave to sweeten or use it in the Oatmeal Cereal Recipe or smoothie recipes. Remember to refrigerate leftovers.

In a medium bowl mix the almond pulp with the carob powder with a fork then add the agave and mix with the fork again until evenly mixed. Then using your hands you can roll small balls then flatten into cookie 2 shapes make sure they are well compacted, spoon desired amount of "creamy filling" which is the coconut oil, in between 2 of the "cookies" and enjoy. If you live where it is very hot and the coconut oil is liquid then you will need to cool it to a solid state. You could also blend the coconut oil with some coconut meat to make a creamy filling too. What I like to use are cute cookie cutters and molds in the shape of hearts and stars. It is easy to press the almond carob mix down, add the coconut oil gently press down then add more carob almond pulp mix and press down firmly, then gently ease it out of the mold or cookie cutter.

This is such a all natural super food and super nutritious dessert/snack because the almonds are alive and living with fully activated enzymes, nutrients and vitamins while the coconut oil has anti-aging properties and is an all natural high quality oil with so many benefits. The super energy really comes through in the super taste of this recipe. Can you imagine a sweet decadent snack/treat that is actually good for you, helps anti-age and beautify you from the inside!? Well now you get to enjoy it and it is real. Kids really love it and you are providing them with the best food on the planet. Adults totally love these too so make some for your friends and teach them all the benefits, they will thank you for it. There is a photo on the cover. An innovative organic living super food dessert! This is my most popular and requested dessert recipe.

Rawinkies

Instead of Carob use 3 to 4 Tablespoons of high quality bee pollen. You will get the yellow color and make this a super food! The bee pollen may have a energetic intense flavor and the coconut oil will smoothen it all out.

8 Servings

2 Cups soaked Almonds, you can also use and substitute 2 Cups soaked Sunflower Seeds if you cannot find or have access to Raw Organic Almonds

2 Cups Water

2 to 3 Tablespoons Bee Pollen to taste

5 Tablespoons Agave

Nutiva Raw Extra Virgin Coconut Oil

Cheesecloth

Small Cookie Cutters

Put the Almonds and Water into the Blend-Tec Blender and blend for 2 to 3 minutes or until the almonds become very small crumb like in size. Pour into Cheesecloth over a large mixing bowl. Squeeze all the almond milk you can out of the almond pulp and save the pulp. Later you can experiment and make them as moist or dry as you like. Save the almond milk to drink, you can add some agave to sweeten or use it in the Oatmeal Cereal Recipe or save it for the smoothies, always refrigerate leftovers.

In a medium bowl mix the almond pulp with the bee pollen with a fork then add the agave and mix with the fork again until evenly mixed. Then using your hands you can roll small balls then flatten into a rectangular shape, spoon desired amount of "creamy filling" which is the coconut oil, make another rectangular "cookie" then spoon the coconut oil in between the two "rectangular cookies" press together and enjoy. If you live where it is very hot and the coconut oil is liquid then you will need to fridge it or cool it to a solid state. You could also blend the coconut oil with some coconut meat to make a creamy filling too. I like to use cookie cutters and molds in the shape of hearts and stars. It is easy to press the almond bee pollen mix down, add the coconut oil then add more almond bee pollen mix press down firmly, then gently ease it out of the mold or cookie cutter.

The bee pollen will have an intense flavor and it has super food quality to it. You should not eat these on an empty stomach because the bee pollen is intense. And don't make them too large because of the intense nature and quality of the bee pollen, you can decrease the bee pollen accordingly if you want to make them larger.

DESSERTS

Pancakes

I decided to put the Pancakes in the Dessert Section because it is sweet and the next two recipes are very similar. Ground Golden Flax Seeds has super energy and health promoting powers. They are a bit "heavy" so you will only want to eat one, they are very satisfying and filling!

2 SERVINGS

1 Cup Golden Flax Seeds
4 Tablespoons of Olive Oil or Coconut Oil in liquid form
2 Tablespoons of Water

Put the golden flax seeds in the Blend-Tec blender and blend into a powder. Then pour into a bowl and mix with the rest. Use a fork and make sure to press down and mix very well until all the flax is coated and the whole mixture is really together. Split the mixture in half, form a ball with your hands and then flatten on a plate and do the same with the other half. Drizzle with Agave and enjoy.

Crepes

4 SERVINGS

1 Cup Golden Flax Seeds
5 Tablespoons of Olive Oil or Coconut Oil in liquid form
6 Tablespoons of Water

Put the golden flax seeds in the Blend-Tec blender and blend into a very fine powder. Pour into a bowl and mix with the rest of the ingredients with a fork then use a spoon and also press down and mix well. Make a medium sized ball with your hands then press down on plate with your hands then a spoon to form a very thin round circular layer. Fill one side with your favorite fruit, any of the dessert creams or fillings then start to carefully roll the crepe. You can use Carob "Chocolate Sauce" which is the 2nd Layer from the Triple Layer Chocolate Cake, more of your choice of dessert creams/fillings or just Agave on top to make it sweet and complete! If you put guacamole or the nacho pine nut cheese sauce inside you will have a Raw Enchilada.

RAWsmores

Pancakes Recipe
Nutiva Extra Virgin Coconut Oil
2nd Layer from the Triple Layer Chocolate Cake Recipe, Page 96
Cinnamon to taste

Using the Pancake Recipe, Page 103, cut the flattened pancakes into small square shapes. Sprinkle some cinnamon on top. In between 2 square layers, add a layer of coconut oil in solid form then a layer of the Carob Pine Nut Sauce which is the 2nd Layer from the Triple Layer Chocolate Cake Recipe. Put together to form a RAWsmore and enjoy!

Baklava

This version is extra refreshing and has a nice light sweet quality. It is so simple and easy too. This should only take a few minutes to make and can be made very quickly, enjoy!

4 Servings

1 Medium Fuji Apple
1 Cup Sunflower Seeds or Walnuts or Pistachios
2 Tablespoons Agave

Use a mandolin to slice the fuji apple into 4 slices. Stack the 4 layers on top of each other on a plate and carefully cut into a square shape with a knife.

In the Blend-Tec blender pour in your choice of nuts, you may soak them but I find that unsoaked ones make this more crunchy, it is up to you along with your choice of nuts. Baklavas have different nuts, the sunflower seeds are the least expensive out of the three and are a very good choice. Blend the nuts until they are very small crumb sized. Pour into a bowl and mix with the agave until well blended.

Using your hands or a spoon, fill in between each layer of apples with the agave nut mixture and pat down with a spoon to compact before adding the next layer on top. Fill all the layers then drizzle with more agave on top, then enjoy! People tell me how amazed they are that this looks and tastes like the baked Baklava version but this one is even fresher and lighter. Photo is on the front cover.

Chocolate Chip Cookies

Imagine a chocolate chip cookie that only takes a few minutes to prepare and it's done. Well imagine no more because here it is!

Cookie:
1 Cup Soaked or Non Soaked Almonds
1 Cup Water
2 Tablespoons Agave
Dash of Cinnamon
1 Cup Ground Golden Flax Seeds

Chocolate Chips:
½ Cup Carob Powder
Small chocolate chip sized pieces of Coconut flesh

This is for when you want to make a quick batch of about 8 chocolate cookies. You can use non soaked Almonds if you do not have any that were soaked but it is better to have soaked ones to make this a living cookie. The above recipe is only if you do not have soaked almonds or almond pulp mixed with agave ready.

Pour the water into the Blend-Tec blender, add all the ingredients and blend until the almonds are a very small crumb size. Pour into a cheesecloth and squeeze all the almond milk into a bowl and set aside the almond milk and almond pulp.

Mix the almond pulp with 2 Tablespoons of agave and a dash of cinnamon. Then make small balls with your hands and flatten into cookie shapes. Compact them to make them stick and stay together. Coat with ground golden flax seeds and place on a plate.

To make the chocolate chips, roll chocolate chip sized coconut bits and pieces into raw organic carob powder until coated then place on top of the cookies, press down so they stay and serve Raw Living Super Nutritious Chocolate Cookies. Moist and delicious. If you use the almond milk you can have cookies and "milk." If you add some carob powder and agave to the almond milk you will have "chocolate milk!"

Ginger Cookies

I loved ginger cookies as a kid, with this recipe you can make ginger bread men and women or even ginger bread houses if you make enough "dough."

8 Servings

- **1 Cup Soaked or Non Soaked Almonds**
- **1 Cup Water**
- **2 Tablespoons Agave**
- **2 Teaspoons of finely grated fresh Ginger**
- **Dash of Cinnamon**
- **1 Cup Ground Golden Flax Seeds**

This recipe is good if you do not have some prepared almond pulp mixed with agave on hand to shape into cookies and you need to make a batch quickly or if you do not have soaked almonds ready you can just use the raw organic almonds in the above recipe to make 8 quick ginger cookies. If you have some almond pulp mixed with agave then just mix in the grated ginger, cinnamon some ground golden flax seed on the outside and then shape and compact into cookies or ginger bread men or women or even ginger bread houses.

To prepare the recipe pour the water into the Blend-Tec blender then add the almonds, agave then blend until the almonds are a very small crumb size. Pour into a cheesecloth and squeeze all the almond milk into a bowl and set aside the almond milk and almond pulp.

Mix the almond pulp with 2 Tablespoons of agave and a dash of cinnamon and 2 teaspoons of grated fresh ginger. Mix well with a fork then make small balls with your hands and flatten into cookie shapes. Compact them to make them stick and stay together. Coat with ground golden flax seeds and place on a plate to serve. The cookies will be moist and delicious. Think of them as being soft batches. You can even drink the almond milk and have cookies and "milk."

VG - balls work best

Energy Bars

*W*hy not make your own fresh wholesome totally organic energy bars the way you like and with super Organic Raw Tibetan Goji Berries. This is super food!

3 to 4 Servings

1 Cup Sunflower Seeds	1 Cup Pumpkin Seeds
1 Cup Pine Nuts	1 Cup Almonds
¼ Cup soaked Buckwheat	Water
¼ Cup Agave	Tibetan Goji Berries

These are great for hiking trips, snacks and to have on hand for some quick good pick me up energy. I have found that using the nuts and seeds dry and not soaked helps to keep them crunchy and they tend to stay together better in this recipe, you have to soak the buckwheat to make them soft. You can choose your choice of the first 5 ingredients to mix, one of my favorite combinations is the sunflower, pumpkin seed, dried Tibetan Goji Berries and soaked buckwheat. Put all the ingredients you choose into the Blend-Tec Blender or food processor and blend for a few seconds. In a bowl mix everything with the agave and a little water to moisten and add some more whole dried Tibetan Goji Berries.

The next step is to compact it enough so that they stay together as an Energy Bar. I like using the various cookie molds because you can really compact them into fun shapes and they work really well. You can also make balls with your hands or use a fork on a plate to make really compacted Energy Bars. After compacting them you can add more energy by allowing them to sit in direct sunlight for a while. Depending on how good you are at compacting and mixing these energy bars, they may or may not stay together so you may want to store them in containers when transporting them.

As a side note one of my favorite quick Trail Mixes is just Pine Nuts with Tibetan Goji Berries. You can add other ingredients of course but I have found this mix to be really satisfying, quick and easy. The creaminess of the pine nuts compliments the sweetness of the Tibetan Goji Berries. Often times in the morning I will put a mix together in a bag and then bring them with me as I head out for the day. It makes the perfect happy energy snack! Remember Tibetan Goji Berries is a super food and I know people will soon discover all the wonderful benefits of them as I am helping to introduce them into the mainstream. They are so delicious and they really make you feel happy!

Tibetan Goji Berry Macaroons

More super food and super desserts. I came up with this recipe when my friend Siva Kami from the Sivananda Yoga Center asked me if I had a Raw Organic Macaroon Cookie recipe, I looked around at the ingredients I had and came up with this amazing one that we both really enjoyed!

8 SERVINGS

2 Fresh Young Coconuts

¼ Cups blended soaked Buckwheat (optional)

Almond Pulp from Almond Milk Recipe mixed with ¼ Cup Agave, Page 71

4 Tablespoons Nutiva Raw Extra Virgin Coconut Oil

¼ Cup Water

¼ Cup Agave

Soaked Tibetan Goji Berries

Finely ground Golden Flax Seeds (optional)

You can make these with Tibetan Goji Berries in the mix or just on top as a garnish. Place all the ingredients into a blender with the water first, coconut flesh next with some coconut water, almond pulp, coconut oil then agave and soaked Tibetan Goji Berries(optional). Blend until a semi smooth chunky consistency. The coconut flesh should be pretty fine and semi smooth In texture then you know you are done blending.

Next using your hands make macaroon size balls and coat with extra almond pulp to make it drier and firmer, you can also use some ground golden flax seeds or blended buckwheat(optional) also, continue to shape into balls after adding the almond pulp or ground flax seeds. Then slightly flatten the macaroon balls with your hands or spoon and add one soaked Tibetan Goji Berry on top for garnish and enjoy!

These will be moist and wet which adds water to your body which is already made of 80% or more of water. Remember the more water you add to your body, and the more liquid you move the better your well being. That is why I also suggest practicing Yoga. If you do Yoga and eat Raw Organic Cuisine you will find that you will turn into a super hero and feel super good about it! These macaroons have so much flavor and energy that you will want to make a bunch. This recipe makes about 10 macaroons.

Mango & Coconut Cream

This one is basic, quick and very easy but so complex and delicious at the same time. I like to make it look like a flower and my clients all love this recipe.

2 SERVINGS

1 Large perfectly ripe Mango

1 Fresh Young Coconut flesh carefully scraped

4 Tablespoons Agave

2 Tablespoons Nutiva Raw Extra Virgin Coconut Oil

½ Cup Pine Nuts

Cinnamon

¼ Cup Water

Blueberries

Soaked Tibetan Goji Berries (soaked 10 minutes)

This is based on one my favorite Thai Dessert. Peel the mango and then cut into long wedge slices and place on a plate.

Put the water into the Blend-Tec Blender first then the scraped coconut flesh, agave, coconut oil, dash of cinnamon and blend until very smooth. Set aside.

Clean the blender jug or use another one and put the water in first, then pine nuts, agave and a dash of cinnamon. Blend until very smooth then pour over the mango slices. Garnish with the blueberries and Tibetan Goji Berries then pour the coconut mixture over the top and enjoy.

Blueberry Mousse

Blueberries are very low in sugar and high in anti-oxidants. Nature's perfect snack! So is this dessert recipe.

2 TO 3 SERVINGS

1 to 2 Bananas
1 Cup Blueberries
Agave to taste
¼ Cup Water

This is the final dessert recipe which is ultra basic and simple yet versatile. I also wanted to wrap up the dessert section with extra variations and suggestions. For this recipe you just mash or blend everything together and serve. By now you should be an expert making pie shells with the Almond Pulp and agave mixture. You can make a quick blueberry pie, small blueberry fruit tarts or make an amazing American Flag Pie!

American Flag Pie: Make the pie crust in a large glass pie pan with the Almond Pulp and agave mixture. Then pour in the first layer with the Strawberry Cream Recipe, then with the Coconut Cream Recipe you can make it extra thick by adding more coconut oil or pine nuts and blend until really smooth then pour over the strawberry layer to form the 2nd layer, then pour in the 3rd and final next layer with this Blueberry Pudding Recipe for a red, white and blue pie! You can go further by making a American Flag design on top with the extra creams on hand.

I love America so much and am so appreciative of all the freedom, spirituality and loving people that make up our truly great country. America is living proof that Unity and Freedom works. Dreams really do come true here and anyone can achieve great success if they work hard and choose the right path. We are so blessed with abundance, wealth and health, my healing mission and aspiration in life is to promote this through Raw Organic Food and being Environmental. This is how I am contributing back to the community, nation and world! It is my way of saying thanks for all the love, support and it truly makes me happy when I can help others in healthy wonderful ways. My PA~RAW~DISE Raw Organic Eco company is how I am going to manifest great healing, awareness, more jobs, opportunities and of course joy. I hope you can support it and please check out the Website for all the great developments and news: http://www.paradise.com.

DESSERTS

SMOOTHIES

Strawberry Tibetan Goji Berry

Kiwi Coconut Lime

Mango Papaya

Coconut Cream

Papaya Berry

Fuzzy Peach

Chocolate Shake

Green Power

SMOOTHIES

Strawberry Tibetan Goji Berry Smoothie

I am so surprised that Tibetan Goji Berries are not as mainstream or common as candy! They are nature's super food and all natural "candy" but with super revitalizing and vibrant health effects. They are known to prevent and fight cancer, have natural anti-aging effects and also have a happiness inducing quality as well. I am doing my best to promote them. Http://www.Extremehealthgoji.com has the BEST!

1 to 2 Servings

1 Fresh Young Coconut
1 Cup Strawberries chopped into small pieces
2 Tablespoons Agave
¼ Cup soaked Tibetan Goji Berries

Carefully scrape the coconut flesh and pour the coconut water into a bowl and take out all the splinters and fibers then pour into the Blend Tec Blender, then add all the rest of the ingredients and blend to desired consistency. If you do not access to fresh young coconuts then you may also use almond milk instead. The Tibetan Goji Berries gives this smoothie such a vibrant unique energetic flavor that will delight you while giving you amazing super vitality.

I know that the more people discover and try Tibetan Goji Berries, the more blissed out they will become! Bliss is one of my favorite Yoga terms. According to Yoga bliss and joy is our all natural state of being and ultimately our real true self. That is why the Raw Organic Living Cuisine is the best diet and choice for returning to our true identity and state of well being on all levels possible.

There is a special photograph on the back cover with the Golden Gate Bridge in the background. This is America's most loved cultural icon and recognized symbol which is very fitting because I hope that this Strawberry Tibetan Goji Berry Smoothie can achieve the same recognition and status soon.

Kiwi Coconut Lime Smoothie

This smoothie is so refreshingly tropical and with the most delightful glowing green color too! The flavor will transport you to the Islands as you relax next to the none-chlorine pool, beach or picnic outing.

1 TO 2 SERVINGS

1 Fresh Young Coconut
2 Kiwis
2 Tablespoons Agave
A few squeezes of Lime

Carefully scrape the coconut flesh and pour the coconut water into a bowl and take out all the splinters and fibers then pour into the Blend-Tec Blender and add all the rest of the ingredients and blend until smooth. You can add a few Tibetan Goji Berries before blending to give this smoothie some nice colors. This is a really great green refreshing Island style drink.

Variations: You can add ½ Cup of Strawberries before blending for a great mix. You can also use pineapple or honey dew melon too. Just a reminder that pineapple and honey dew melons are considered to be high glycemic and high sugar index fruit. But we use them very sparingly in my recipes and the pineapple has such amazing digestive live enzyme qualities that I like to use it and include it in the recipes. It also has the great flavor and Island Vibe. The best ones I have found come from Maui, Hawaii and Rainbow Grocery carries this perfect pineapple. Hawaii is one of the most magical and perfect places on Earth, it is definitely one of my favorites and I have had very enlightening experiences there every time I visit. The last time I was in Hawaii there was a great article about a new Fruit Grower on the East side of Oahu, he travels around the world to locate rare tantalizing exotic fruit and then grows them organically on Oahu. What a great business and concept I thought, I would love to do that some day as well.

Mango Papaya Smoothie

This is a winning combination of two super fruits. Exotic, tropical, creamy all in one smoothie!

2 SERVINGS

1 Fresh Young Coconut
1 Mango
1 Papaya
2 Tablespoons Agave

Carefully scrape the coconut flesh and pour the coconut water into a bowl and take out all the splinters and fiber then pour into the Blend-Tec Blender and add all the rest of the ingredients and blend until smooth. If you do not have access to fresh young coconuts then you may also use almond milk instead. You can add a few soaked Tibetan Goji Berries before blending to give this smoothie some nice colors. A little Tibetan Goji Berry adds a nice color and will keep you happy all day long! For a sunset looking type of smoothie you can add some fresh cranberry juice or blended strawberries on top. This is a very nice pick me up during lunch break or even for breakfast. The papaya has super enzymes, is great for digestion and will keep you beautiful and energized.

Coconut Cream Smoothie

We can go coconuts over this sweet nectar. Coconuts have a very high electrolyte content, natural sweet quality and is the ultimate in smooth creamy smoothies.

1 Fresh Young Coconut flesh and water
2 Tablespoons Agave
A Sprinkle or two of Cinnamon to taste

Carefully scrape the coconut flesh and pour the coconut water into a bowl and take out all the splinters and fiber then pour into the Blend-Tec Blender then add all the rest of the ingredients and blend until smooth. If you do not access to fresh young coconuts then you must find some because this recipe calls for it! You can add a few soaked Tibetan Goji Berries(optional) before blending to give this smoothie some nice colors. A little Tibetan Goji Berry will keep you happy all day long! This one is simple, easy and one of my favorites because it is so naturally creamy.

Papaya Berry Smoothie

Living enzymatic nutrition never tasted so good The dream is real and so is this smoothie. Bliss in a blender!

1 TO 2 SERVINGS

1 Fresh Young Coconut
1 Papaya from Hawaii
¼ Cup Strawberry
¼ Cup Raspberries
¼ Cup Blueberries
2 Tablespoons Agave

Carefully scrape the coconut flesh and pour the coconut water into a bowl and take out all the splinters and fibers then pour into the Blend-Tec Blender then add all the rest of the ingredients and blend to desired consistency. If you do not have access to fresh young coconuts then you can use almond milk. You can add a few soaked Tibetan Goji Berries(optional) before blending to give this smoothie some nice colors. The sweetness of the papaya gives a nice contrast to the tart flavors of the strawberries and raspberries. Blueberries have one of the highest amounts of anti-oxidants! This will transport you to the Islands as you relax with this smoothie.

Fuzzy Peach

*W*hen I bite into a Peach, it is like biting into the best Summer memories of a lifetime! Peaches have that special quality that absorbs all the Summer time sun and fun.

1 TO 2 SERVINGS

1 Peach
1 Pear
1 Apricot
¼ Cup Water
1 Tablespoon Agave

Pour the water into the Blend-Tec blender first then add all the ingredients and blend until smooth.

Variations: Add some strawberries or fresh cranberry juice for a nice sunset color. Or even some pineapple for some extra zing.

Chocolate Shake

A frothy "milky" creamy chocolate shake with no chocolate in it! We use Raw Organic Carob Powder instead. Chocolate lovers will celebrate with this recipe!

1 TO 2 SERVINGS

1 Fresh Young Coconut flesh and water or 1 ½ Cups Almond Milk or other nut milk
4 Tablespoons of Carob Powder
2 to 3 Tablespoons Agave to taste

Carefully scrape the coconut flesh and pour the coconut water into a bowl and take out all the splinters and fibers then pour into the Blend-Tec Blender and add all the rest of the ingredients and blend to desired consistency. If you do not have access to fresh young coconuts then you can use almond milk or other nut milk. This is one vegan Chocolate Shake that is so super creamy and amazing. There is a nice photo on the cover with the famous Golden Gate Bridge in the background.

For a Raw "Coffee" or Raw "Mocha" or Raw "Latte" e-mail me or check out the Rawinten.com website! I do have healthier substitutions and versions for people who want a healthy alternative.

Always check the Rawinten.com website for new recipes, updates, news and developments and e-mail me with any questions, comments, suggestions, etc. and I will be more than happy to answer all them personally. I want to provide you with the best Raw Organic experience ever!

Pina Colada

*F*resh coconut and pineapple bring this Hawaiian Style health drink to life! I always loved the sweet and sour flavor combinations of these two.

1 TO 2 SERVINGS

1 Cup Pineapple
1 Fresh Young Coconut with flesh and water
1 Banana

Blend all the ingredients in the Blend-Tec blender and serve with a tiny umbrella! I have seen tiny umbrellas made out of bits and pieces of fruit, etc. Let you imagination and creativity show.

Variations: Add a few soaked Tibetan Goji Berries, or strawberries or even an orange.

Green Power Smoothie

*F*or a super alkalizing, oxygenating green drink try this recipe! It also has the incredible Vita Mineral Green Powder made by Health Force Nutritionals. They recommend on their label to eat more Raw Organic foods and to help balance the body's Ph with green foods. Their Website: Healthforce.com

1 TO 2 SERVINGS

2 Kiwis

1 Pear

1 Banana

1 Orange

Some Pineapple chunks

Some Sunflower Sprouts

1 to 2 Teaspoons Teaspoon Vita Mineral Green Powder

Squeeze of Lime (optional)

Put all the ingredients into the Blend-Tec blender and blend until smooth. It is always good to drink a green power smoothie every now and then to get all the green power. With Vita Mineral Green Powder you know you are getting a lot of the best greens. Now you can be eco green and drink green and we will all have a more harmonious, healthy, peaceful loving world. But the adventure is just beginning! Eating and drinking pure healthy nutritious foods is only one aspect of a whole person and being, although it is the MOST important aspect of all. You also need to exercise, have proper breathing, proper relaxation, proper rest, meditation, nice friends, good relationships, positive thinking, fresh clean air and water and more time in nature. I find that Yoga is one of the best ways to accomplish all of the above. I have more food for thought in the following pages and it we will all go further together.

Please contact Health Force Nutritional orders and information, truly the BEST!

1-800-357-2717

Quotes

There is a lot of information that I want to share with you. They are all recent, new and up to the minute Raw necessary facts. It is all very important and interesting. Awareness is the key to winning and awakening to the truth. I have listed inspiring quotes, books, ideas, websites and news so enjoy!

"I give you every seed bearing plant that is upon all the earth, and every tree that has seed bearing fruit, they shall be yours for food."– God

"I chose you and appointed you to go and bear fruit – fruit that will last." – Jesus said to His followers

"Let Thy Food be Thy Medicine and thy Medicine be thy Food" – Hippocrates the "Father" of modern medicine

"Nothing will benefit human health and increase chances for survival of life on Earth as much as the evolution to a vegetarian diet."– Albert Einstein

"My best year of track competition was the first year I ate a vegan diet" – Carl Lewis Olympian Champion

"Every time we eat we are making a powerful choice. Thousands of people every day in the United States are waking up to the effects that their food choices have on animals, the planet and their health."– Nathan Runkle, Mercy for Animals Director

"The costs of mass producing cattle, poultry, pigs, sheep and fish to feed our growing population… Include hugely inefficient use of freshwater and land, heavy pollution from livestock feces…and spreading destruction of the forests of which much of our planet's life depends"– Time Magazine 11/8/99

"I consistently find that many of the spiritual processes are amplified with live foods: meditation, contemplation, flexibility in Yoga…and more experiences of the Divine…Living Foods accelerates the flow of cosmic energy in the body." – Gabriel Cousens M.D.

"You are what you eat!"– Common but truthful saying

"We all have the Buddha nature within and have come back to save all sentient beings" – Buddha

"RAW is WAR spelled backwards because we are choosing PEACE!"– Bryan Au

"Enjoy and savior each and every morsel as your spiritual practice of being in the present" – Thicht Nhat Hahn

"Have compassion for all beings" –The Honorable 14th Dalai Lama

Many people are attracted to and start the Raw Organic Gourmet Cuisine for many reasons. For some it is their: spiritual path, a new delicious curiosity, a challenge to see how Raw and healthier one can become each day, desire to lose or gain healthy weight, naturally anti-age and rejuvenate, gain energy and strength, an interesting exciting new cuisine, a way to be more creative, one of the ways to save people's health and the planet, save time, increase joy and happiness naturally, a new way to enjoy and promote organic food, because Celebrities are into it, because it makes sense, because it is fun…the list keeps going on and on forever. For me I would have to say that it is a mix of all of the above and more. I have also solved the Acrylamide problem and have e-mailed everyone I could that is doing research Into solving this. I am also trying to reach out to doctors and researchers to do more research on the benefits of the Raw Organic Gourmet Cuisine so that more people will get awareness, education and have access to all the healthy truths! Nature and Organic food is not a fad, it has been around much longer than say the Atkins Diet for example!

I feel like all the doctors took the Hippocrates oath and so they also should follow his "Let food be thy medicine and they medicine be thy food" principle. I have been contacted by hospitals interested in this cuisine. The fact is that the Raw Organic Gourmet Cuisine can prevent and treat many modern illnesses, diseases and health problems. I am trying to make it more mainstream and as acceptable as say inorganic processed food or destructive fast food. I would like more people to have access and awareness so at the very least they can make the best choices possible. There is one famous raw food chef that keeps saying that this is the cuisine that everyone wishes for but doesn't know exists. I have also been contacted by the California Culinary Academy and by Upton Catering as they were very interested in my cuisine and food. I am trying very hard to get the Raw Organic Cuisine into the mainstream, to have it be taught at Culinary Academies and in schools.

One of my goals is to have it available in the school cafeteria system. I wish I had access to it as a kid growing up instead of the bad junk foods they served at school. They used to microwave frozen artificial preservative laden carcinogenic "food" in the plastic wrapper so it was melted and fused with the "food!" We have come a long way since and I would hope that children would now be allowed to have access to fresh, healthy raw organic food. Some of the food can still be "warmed up" using their cafeteria steamers and still be considered raw organic living foods as long as it is under 114 degrees. After this book comes out and people try my recipes I hope they will be more open and accepting so that everyone can enjoy and have access to good quality healthy organic raw food and cuisine. Please contact and e-mail me to have your school carry Raw Organic goodness. I am ready to cater to any school cafeteria in the country. My recipes only look and taste like favorite junk foods and comfort foods but are made with the highest quality fresh organic healthy ingredients, purity and are the best for your health and for growing kids! As you can see they are also time and cost efficient as well. The foods may be lightly steamed or heated as long as it is below 114 degrees as it is considered to be living and alive still. I have found that kids really love all of my recipes and they like to prepare it too, their parents love how it is raw organic goodness and they always order extra portions for themselves and for their kids. Often times their kids would eat most of what they ordered, they were so pleased and happy to see their children naturally be attracted to and enjoy all natural organic raw healthy food. They would then tell me what extra portions they would like to order and what their kid's favorites were. So many people asked me for my recipes and techniques that it motivated me to write this recipe book. I have a very successful catering and delivery business that was saving people time and money while they got to enjoy the best cuisine. Now I want to expand and share it with the rest of the country and world. I want to continue by providing To-Go Franchises, Restaurants and a packaged food line. I am also always creating new recipes everyday.

Whatever reasons you have for enjoying this special Raw Organic cuisine believe me that you are indeed enjoying the best and being able to do the most healing for your own health and for the Earth. Here is a list of some celebrities and famous people that are Raw Organic Gourmet Living Cuisine and Living Foods people while others are vegetarian and vegan:

Alicia Silverstone and Woody Harrelson are the super hero activists that are really leading the way in this movement, Demi Moore in preparation for her film Charlie's Angels where she surprised everyone with her youthful rejuvenated new Raw Organic Cuisine look, Lisa Bonet is totally into it, Michael Richards who I met and turned onto Raw, Super Model Carol Alt, the Barbie Twins, Bill Cosby, Alec Baldwin, Sting and many more!

Vegans and Vegetarians: Carl Lewis, Angela Basset, Prince, Kim Basinger, Pamela Anderson, Paul McCartney, Shania Twain, Martina Navratilova I was her ball boy once at the Manhattan Beach Country Club when I was a teenager, Jack LaLanne, Albert Einstein, Edwin Moses, Robert Parish, Billie Jean King, Russel Simmons, Mahatma Ghandi, Ziggy Marley, Cesar Chavez, Steve Jobs, Moby, Toby Mcguire, Morissey, Peter Tosh.

There are 2 great Vegetarian Starter Kits that are Free, one is by Peta their Website: Goveg.com and the other is Mercy for Animals: Mercyforanimals.org. They are both really great in that they have the full spectrum of being light and informative on one hand but also can be very intense and graphic on the other. It is all to create the all important awareness and education that we all need about the truth of what is going on everyday. We are all so important as individuals and all of our choices have either a negative or very healing loving positive impact in our world that become more amplified everyday. Lets become part of the solution and not the pollution! There is so much more information and there is always new research and data coming out. Basically we humans are designed to be herbivores in every way, we were meant to eat fruits, nuts and vegetables. Just because we are able to eat other things does not mean we should, the very real possible future of disease, cancer and other health problems await those that eat processed foods, inorganic and unnatural foods. Some people may feel like they will miss out on their favorite foods but with my recipes they can enjoy more, they taste "meaty", creamy, decadent and they will become even healthier instead of sicker with time and age. Being able to anti-age and stay young from the Raw Organic Cuisine is a reality. These are real facts and I encourage people to do as much research as they can, there are many great books and free information on the Internet that will shock, surprise and enlighten you. Why not choose a healthy happy life? Health is the ultimate wealth. You will also be able to save the environment and create a much more peaceful, loving harmonious world for everyone. By taking part in this book and recipes you are able to be a super hero while enjoying really great recipes and food in a fun quick and easy way. This is the best fast food possible. I will save you time, money and you will get so many rewards as a result. Yes you can save your health and the world by the way you eat!

Recommended Books

The Rainbow Green Live Food Cuisine, Gabriel Cousens M.D., North Atlantic Books

Conscious Eating, Gabriel Cousens M.D., North Atlantic Books

Eating For Beauty, David Wolfe, Maui Brothers Publishing

Raw Power, Stephen Arlin, Maui Brothers Publishing

Nature's First Law: The Raw Food Diet, Stephen Arlin, Fouad Dini, David Wolfe, Maui Brothers Publishing

The Sprouting Book, Anne Wigmore, Avery Publishing Group Inc.

Surviving into the 21 Century, Victorias Kulvinskas M.S., Century Publishing

Enzyme Nutrition, Edward Howell, Avery Publishing

Sprouts the Miracle Food, Steve Meyerowitz, Sproutman Publications

Choices For Our Future, Ocean Robbins and Sol Soloman, Book Publishing Company

Diet for a New America, John Robbins, Book Publishing Company

The Food Revolution, John Robbins, Book Publishing Company

Save Our Planet, Diane MacEachern, Dell Publishing

Autobiography of a Yogi, ParamahansaYogananda, Self Realization Fellowship

Highly Recommended Websites

http://www.rammedearthworks.com
http://www.rammedearth.com

I am promoting Rammed Earth homes as the best Raw Organic All Natural Homes available today! They are truly gorgeous, amazing and all natural. I think they should be the standard in modern day home building because they are earthquake, fire and termite proof! I have been working with the director of the Treasure Island Development and he agrees with me that it would be a great idea to have a Rammed Earth Home on Treasure Island as a Tourist Attraction. My concept is to have the most Eco, Raw Organic home possible so that people and tourists can pay admission to tour the home with all the latest cutting edge Eco and Environmental technologies available today. It would be totally solar and wind powered off the grid, display all the latest Eco technologies such as electric bikes from ZAPZ.OB and hopefully soon Hydrogen Fuel Cell Cars from ZAPZ.OB, eco flooring and furniture, products, etc. The EPA reports that most homes have more toxins and pollution inside than the air outside, this is due to outgassing from glues, carpet, furniture, particle board, paint, toxic cleaners, etc. Please look up "Outgassing" on Google.com for all the eye opening facts and information, they will surprise and startle you with how much pollution conventional homes have inside. The EPA reports that the pollution inside the home can be 70% higher than outside, that children and people's health are being seriously affected and compromised and there is a lot more to find out about. I want people to be aware and to educate themselves with these facts. But there are solutions.

The Rammed Earth Home would have literally no outgassing or toxins of any sort because it is entirely organic and all natural with actual cleaner air inside the home than outside. Treasure Island is isolated which makes all the built in safety features so attractive, but there will be buses and ferries bringing tourists directly to Treasure Island. It will be one of the biggest tourist attractions in San Francisco and this project will be highly successful. I am currently looking for Angel Investors and interested parties to help me build a totally Raw Organic Rammed Earth Model Home and Tourist Attraction, people can pay admission to tour the home and also eat Raw Organic Gourmet Cuisine at the café inside while learning about how to be more eco and natural while saving money and the environment. Presently there are only a few cafes, cafeterias and one or two restaurants on Treasure Island, with all the new expected tourists, increased housing and large present population there, a Raw Organic Café and Restaurant would be highly successful. So much pollution and waste will be solved and people will be able to see it done in a practical, upscale, desirable manner. This Rammed Earth home will also serve as a model for complete eco housing packages that people can order from us directly.

Please e-mail me about this exciting lucrative development project.

http://www.who.int/foodsafety/publications/chem/acrylamide_june2002/en/

The above Website addresses the very real problem of Acrylamide in food, one that the Raw Organic Living Cuisine has already deliciously solved, there is no need to look for a solution when one already exists. I have e-mailed everyone I could about how Raw Living Food already solves the Acrylamide problem but have yet to receive any responses. I am hoping to change that, here is even more information:

http://www.cspinet.org/new/200206251.html
http://vm.cfsan.fda.gov/~dms/acrydata.html
http://www.cfsan.fda.gov/~dms/acrydino.html
http://www.hc-sc.gc.ca/food-aliment/cs-ipc/chha-edpcs/e_acrylamide_and_food.html
http://veggie.org/veggie/10veggie.shtml
http://www.thegardendiet.com/news/demi.html
http://www.naturalhealthweb.com/articles/morgan1.html
http://abclocal.go.com/ktrk/health/111203_health_rawdiet.html

The above Website demonstrates how you can lose weight on the Raw Diet but also demonstrates what can happen when people do not know how to eat a balanced Raw Diet! It is obvious that they were eating random food, did not read Gabriel Cousens M.D. books, did not do the research at all. Like with everything you must do the research and also eat a balanced meal according to your goals and individual body's needs. We all have different body types with different calorie consumption and activities. My recipes and this book solves all of these problems in a delicious gourmet satisfying way, if only these people had my recipes and this book! I am about educating people and creating awareness. The RAW diet is so amazing and beautiful when done right. Gas is from improper food combining, not transitioning or eating right. There is a correct way to doing everything, with my book and Gabriel Cousens the doctor who has done the research, you can find out how. Also the media likes to give both sides of the story but does not always give the complete picture. They do not mention the Organic aspect enough, the very real Acrylamide problem and prevention and treatment of disease that the Raw Organic Cuisine addresses and solves in a fun delicious way. Here is more information:

http://umanitoba.fitdv.com/new/articles/article.html?artid=391

The above article is a little better but does not give the complete picture, articles have to sound and be interesting but if you read well documented research from Gabriel Cousens M.D. you will get all the medical and scientific facts.

Through my personal experiences I have met with people and found that the Raw Organic Cuisine can and has prevented many modern diseases while helping people to heal and be on the path to a cure for their conditions. One of the main reasons is because at the very least the body is allowed to function properly because there is no toxins or pesticides because everything is Raw and Organic, most articles do not mention this important fact! The body and all its functions are allowed to realign to its natural healing powers. Also avoiding acrylamide and many other things allows the body to concentrate on healing and functioning properly while boosting the immune system. Also the Raw Organic Cuisine adds the most amount of oxygen, water, is the most alkalizing and balanced in PH if done properly and yes it does add more enzymes which are the building blocks of life and cells, that is why I use Miso and a lot of greens in my recipes as they have these beneficial effects. The media and population is still learning, my mission is to educate and create more awareness. Yoga used to be considered too hippy or radical but is now mainstream and is one of the largest successful growing industries in America today. Once people try something new and get very real tangible noticeable positive benefits, then they will become convinced and will want to learn and try more. The Raw Organic Cuisine is so beneficial on so many levels and is still in the learning and transition stage like how Yoga was not too long ago. The Raw Organic Cuisine deserves to be mainstream and people also deserve more access to it. There are even published medical reports done that revealed that when we eat Raw Organic food that our body does not attack it with white blood cells first to identify it. When we eat cooked foods this happens and lowers our immunity. I am not saying you can never eat any cooked foods, do try to eat Organic! We will always have cooked food cravings and will want to eat cooked foods but at least make sure it is organic. That is why I designed my recipes and cuisine to look and taste "cooked" to satisfy these cravings while giving you all the Raw Organic health benefits. I have yet to meet anyone that was completely 100% eating only cooked food or 100% eating only Raw Organic food either, most people eat a combination of the two in varying degrees. Although it is impressive to be 100% Raw Living and Organic, for most people it is a challenge and you should do the necessary research to come up with the best plan for your needs. Remember it may take some time to transition into, my main point is it should be a natural fun process and decision, many people will naturally and progressively become 100% while others will have varying combinations. Gabriel Cousens actually did research and has found that a 80% Raw Organic Living Food and 20% Organic Cooked Food diet is the most optimal for most people. People ask me what I think about it all the time and you can e-mail me with your questions. I think steaming or warming up some foods and soups when eating cooked food is fine just let it be under 114 degrees. But the Raw Organic Cuisine is so delicious and you will feel so much better that most people will continue and become 90% Raw to 10% Cooked and then even 100% Raw Living Food. There is no requirement and you should do what is most enjoyable and beneficial for your health and the Earth. Through my experiences I know you will enjoy the Raw adventure and will want to learn more and eat more Raw. Yoga is very similar in the beginning, it is a new worthy challenge and practice, but is so much fun and the more you do it the greater you feel about life and yourself. Then you naturally get more into it, the same goes for Raw Organic Cuisine. Here are some interesting personal testimonials about how it has helped people and how it can help with certain diseases:

http://www.shazzie.com/raw/transformation/jaime.shtml

http://www.thepeacefulplace.com/celltech/articles/autism.html

http://www.americanfreepress.net/Alternative_Health/Industrial_Poisons_Can_Be_Crip/industrial_poisons_can_be_crip.html

The latest research on Parkinson's Disease is that it is linked to pesticides. Organic Raw Cuisine does not have any pesticides. "A study at Stanford University reported in May 2000 questioned 496 individuals during their diagnosis for Parkinson's disease about pesticide exposure in the home. It was found that people who had been exposed to pesticides were twice as likely to develop Parkinson's disease as people not exposed to pesticides." Also with Rammed Earth homes there is no pollution of outgassing of toxins which is one of many great reasons to promote and to build them. I believe it should be and can be the next big new industry in America and can create many new jobs while saving the environment and everyone's health.

http://www.rawfoodlife.com/

http://www.cancertutor.com/Cancer/RawFood.html

http://bibleplus.org/health/rawfood.htm

http://www.falconblanco.com/health/alimentation/rawfood1.htm

The above article reveals people's different needs. But also the benefits of the Raw Organic Cuisine, my purpose and intent is to make it more decadent, enjoyable, look and taste like your favorite cooked comfort and junk foods so that you can enjoy this cuisine and stay away from the other destructive unhealthy junk or fast foods out there. And my recipes help you to stick with something that is truly good for you and the environment on many levels. The secret of how to come up with

Raw Organic Recipes? I'll tell you, you have to become more Raw! The more you do it the more new recipes will pop into your head, there is no way to just sit and try to think of new recipes, they just happen spontaneously. There is so much more information on the Internet and I would urge you to read Gabriel Cousens M.D. then do all the research you can on the Internet. I know you will find there is a lot to learn and benefit from the Raw Organic Cuisine. A whole new world, adventure and lifestyle awaits you that will can bring you more joy, vitality, energy and happiness. You will find some personal opinions or some negative information here and there but there are way more benefits, a lot more conclusive positive medical research and data that is out there for you to learn from. With this book you can do it in the most delicious and fun way!

http://www.diagnose-me.com

http://www.diagnose-me.com/treat/T160798.html

The above Website links are very interesting and my friend on the Big Island of Hawaii is running it from his home in Hawaii. He always recommends people do the Raw Organic Cuisine Diet in order to overcome their conditions after they fill out the questionnaire. It is a helpful Website and many high profile people use it for confidentiality and privacy purposes. It lists: In a study where the average intake of uncooked food comprised 62% of calories ingested, 80% of those who smoked abstained spontaneously. [*South Med J 1985 Jul;78(7): pp.841-4*]. A similar result was found for drug abusers and alcoholics so eating a Raw Organic Diet helps your body to detox and also purify to the point where it will recognize toxins and will naturally abstain and it will naturally stop using them and it helps in controlling addictions. To me it is proof that our body is naturally attracted to and wants radiant health. When we allow it and feed it what it really needs and wants then all the pieces come together, the healing and health aspects all combine to assist us. In combination with Yoga you will get the best results. With his Website you also have access to the advice of a team of live doctors that review each case and questionnaire result. I will list more interesting Websites:

http://www.karlloren.com/diet.htm

http://www.treeoflife.nu You can order all of Gabriel Cousens Books directly from his incredible Tree Of Life Rejuvenation Center in Patagonia, Arizona!

http://www.rawguru.com Enter the Coupon Code: **RawInTen** for your special discounts, promotional specials and free gifts with purchases just for my special readers.

You may order Blend-Tec Blenders from Rawguru.com they are very nice to give my special readers a great discount and free gifts with purchases. They will have more discounts and promotions the more we support them. They really do have the best deals and equipment on the Internet. They pay for the tax and shipping on top of giving us great discounts so there are no extra charges, just great deals and savings. They are doing this because they really want to promote raw organic living cuisine and let people have access to more health and joy in their lives.

http://www.commonvision.org

http://www.fresh-network.com Great Raw Website from England.

http://www.voiceyourself.com Woody Harrelson's great Website!

I have a series or popular Yoga Articles that are published on the Internet and wanted to include one of them. I have found that the Raw Organic Cuisine defintely improves and furthers my Yoga practice. I gained much more flexibilty, deeper meditations, positive thinking and other super benefits. I hope you enjoy the article:

http://www.yogaforyou.ca/a_4_int_adv.html

Recommended Raw Organic Living Businesses in San Francisco

As you can tell that this book primarily is centered around San Francisco. This is because this truly is one of the best cities to live in the world. The air is clean, the organic produce is awesome and the Raw Living Foods scene is thriving here. I have became friends with so many super elevated cool people here that everyday is literally an adventure. The Raw Living Community here is so active, supportive and loving that I feel the most nurtured and am so grateful for all my friendships and connections. I have traveled all around this great world and have found San Francisco to be the most enchanting, spiritual and happening city on the planet. The art, culture, diversity, open mindedness of San Francisco make it the most unique and special place in my heart and on Earth. So I encourage you to please visit and when you do please go these great Raw Living Foods Restaurants:

PA~RAW~DISE Raw Organic Cuisine Restaurant

587 Post Street @ Taylor

San Francisco, CA 94120

http://www.Rawinten.com

http://www.Parawdise.com

Now you can come visit me and my new Raw Organic Restaurant in San Francisco and enjoy all the amazing recipes from RAW IN TEN MINUTES at PA~RAW~DISE Restaurant on Union Square! It is the only 100% Raw Organic Vegan Restaurant in the World! We will also have totally new never before seen amazing Gourmet Creations on the Menu with specials too! I want the menu to be totally different and a surprise everyday so you get all the best new creations and innovations in the most delicious gourmet Raw Organic fantasy restaurant possible. It will be the best in the World and will have waterfalls, koi ponds, orchids, fine art and furnishings from around the World, it will be the best dining experience in your life. A true center for awakening, rejuvenation and relaxation, every night we will also have special performances, live entertainment, singers, art openings, film screenings, events, lectures, yoga, and more! So please come, visit and enjoy! We will plan on opening in May or June and we also have a special RAW TOUR Package for tourists and visitors so please e-mail me for all the information and details at: rawbryan@earthlink.net and you can also join my Yahoo Group to get all the updates and information too! The dream and fantasy is real!

Café Gratitude

2400 Harrison Street @ 20th Street

San Francisco, CA 94110

(415)824-4652

http://www.withthecurrent.com

Café Gratitude is a great community restaurant and has a great vibe. Good organic raw living food and reasonable prices. Everyone is so nice and grateful! I for one am super grateful for their super good food and positive energy. Nice crowd and location too.

Be on the look out for my PA~RAW~DISE Raw Organic Restaurant Coming SOON to San Francisco. It will be a total eco jungle theme Parawdise setting with a lot of plants and vines, orchids, water falls and you will feel transported to a realm of total relaxation and rejuvenation. It will literally be the most innovative and incredible oasis and restaurant dining experience in San Francisco. I have several good locations available and I am currently open to investors, RAW Living Food Catering, events, consultations, lectures, interviews, etc.

Please e-mail me at:

Bryan@rawinten.com

And check out my Websites:

http://www.Parawdise.com & http://www.Rawinten.com for bigger color photos of the Recipes, exciting Raw Organic Living developments and news. And join my Yahoo Group for free to post your messages and comments: http://health.groups.yahoo.com/group/pa-raw-dise

Please also shop at and support Rainbow Grocery for being the best in the world and for doing it right. They are my most favorite store and I recommend them 100%. Tell them that Bryan of PA~RAW~DISE sent you and that you found about them in Raw In Ten Minutes.

Rainbow Grocery

1745 Folsom Street

San Francisco, CA 94103

(415)863-0620

http://www.rainbow.coop

Rainbow Grocery also publishes the best monthly Free Magazine/Newsletter I have ever seen. It has all the new organic and eco information with up to date nutrition and news. All with an organic and enlightened sensibility that is very uplifting to read. It is titled *Taste For Life*.

I would like to share some quotes and great information from their latest December 2004 issue which is also the month that this book is published. In the editor's note they talk about how "Play is not a luxury but rather a necessity, especially as modern life becomes increasingly complicated and sometimes downright grim." Well I think the Raw Organic Cuisine gives us every opportunity to "play" with food. Once you reach a certain level of expertise you are able to move among the ingredients and to use them with a sense of freedom and creativity. With love and imagination guiding you and your hands, you are able to play with the food in a way where it becomes an act of love and creation. Many people have told me that preparing raw organic food is so relaxing for them. Part of the reason why is because fruit and vegetables actually have a slightly higher vibration than we do so there is a definite exchange of energies occurring when we are preparing raw organic vegetarian food. There are books that have special photography that shows the "aura" of organic fruits and vegetables and inorganic ones. The energy and increased vibration of the organic ones were very obvious and magnified. The organic fruits and vegetables are actually able to absorb our tension, worries, stress and interchange them with positive relaxing ZEN like energies. When I mention that we can "play" with the food I mean that in a symbolic and creative way. I don't mean we are throwing it around or having food fights, but rather that we are not "working" or "struggling" with the food or process. That is what makes my recipes so enjoyable. They are almost too easy and lots of fun. With beautiful results that will please anyone that gets to enjoy them. Raw organic cuisine give us opportunities to "play" in a useful, safe and productive way.

Their next article is "Healing Holiday Spices" written by Braddock Ray on page 23, the article continues by stating that "the aromatic spices were once worth their weight in gold". This is very true because throughout history herbs and spices had to travel from very far exotic locations. In modern times we are blessed with having everything instantly available at our fingertips. They start to mention great facts like how cinnamon helps to regulate blood sugar and cholesterol among people with Type II Diabetes. While Cayenne and ginger are thermogenic, meaning they increase metabolism and help burn fat faster, which is great for people who want to lose weight. There is apparently a compound in raw ginger that is called "shagoal" and it is strong enough to kill cold viruses. This is all great useful information since we use these very same ingredients in many of the recipes! I just would like to mention more information that they have in their chart about these same great ingredients for your extra knowledge. This is all food for thought!

Cayenne also treats arthritis, cramps, muscle pain, heals ulcers, helps regulate blood pressure, supports circulation, lung problems and varicose veins. They have a recipe for an infusion and tincture.

But I am a big believer in eating these ingredients which makes them much more enjoyable and fun to use while receiving all the plentiful benefits.

Cinnamon treats bronchitis, colds, coughs, fever, gas, indigestion, infections, intestinal spasms, sore throat, diarrhea, menstrual pain, ulcers and yeast infections. They suggest consuming a teaspoon a day to help treat any of the above.

Turmeric treats hepatitis, indigestion, infections, helps treat Alzheimer's disease, arthritis, asthma, athlete's foot, breast and colon cancer, carpal tunnel syndrome, heart disease, cholesterol, menstrual pain, psoriasis and yeast infections, they suggest taking turmeric supplements or eating one teaspoon daily. I have plenty of delicious recipes that use organic turmeric.

There are just two more articles that I would like to quote and write about because they happen to directly affect us. The next article written by Marcia Zimmerman, Med, CN on page 27 is titled "Enzyme Power." In the article it states "As stressful lifestyle and unhealthful diets have increasingly become the norm, digestive problems are on the rise. Currently an estimated 58 percent of Americans suffer from some type of digestive disorder. Eating on the run or eating late in the evening can result in inadequate enzyme production, which leads to digestive disorders and increased inflammation. Improving enzyme function while modifying lifestyle can alleviate these disorders and may completely eliminate them."

It continues with "Critical Catalysts, enzymes, a major class of proteins, are the workhorses of the body. "No mineral, vitamin, or hormone can do any work without enzymes," according to Edward Howell, MD who pioneered enzyme therapy in this country. Encoded by DNA, enzymes are responsible for regulating all cellular activity, activating growth and repair, and eliminating toxins."

Thankfully Raw Organic and Living Foods contains the most amount of enzymes because they are not cooked or destroyed by heat. Then the article states "As we grow older, the body's ability to produce enzymes decreases, so that we cannot digest food as effectively. Raw foods contain natural enzymes that assist digestion. But processing with high heat and prolonged cooking can destroy most enzymes. Unfortunately, the American diet consists primarily of processed foods, many of them prepared at high temperatures. In addition, toxins in synthetic pesticides disturb enzyme systems in the body. "Eating only organic pesticide-free food is one way to maintain and restore your enzyme systems," says enzyme researcher Anthony J. Cichoke, DC. Selecting organic foods locally grown and in season helps increase your consumption of healthy raw foods, while reducing the possibility of encountering mold or bacteria on foods transported from great distances or stored for long periods of time." So as you can see eating fresh organic Raw fruit, vegetables and nuts has greater impact on your health than we all realized. While growing up I had no idea or any concept or access to this kind of truth, facts and information! As a kid I would microwave anything and everything then just stuff it down with even more junk food. But now there are very real healthy alternatives like my raw organic living "junk food" remember it only looks and tastes like it but is really raw organic super healthy foods!

There is so much more information and goodness to learn about. I am so glad that you have access to this information and to this book. Please teach others so they have opportunities to learn and benefit too. You would be surprised how many people have no idea or clue about any of the above information. As a kid and teenager I know that I did not and was lucky enough to meet the right people and read the right books early on before this type of information was more available or becoming as mainstream and accepted as it is now. Who knows how long it would have taken me to find out, with knowledge the sooner you get the information and facts the better because you can start to take the right action. It took a lot of personal research, books and Yoga to lead me to certain truths. A lot of people do not have access to these facts and truths and may have to suffer as a result, that is why I am doing this and promoting this to end the suffering and needless health problems. Prevention, education and awareness is so vital and essential. In Yoga we are always reminding ourselves of how health is our true wealth and birthright. Without it life can become challenging but there are always ways to solve challenges, always look for real solutions and never give up. Lets rise up to meet challenges, solve modern problems, make the right choices everyday. Now there are delicious, easy, quick fun easy ways to do so! Thank you for reading this book, I truly hope you enjoyed it as much as I did in writing and creating it and I hope you had a lot of fun. It does make a great gift and so please share the gift of health with all of your friends, family and loved ones.

Why Choose Organic?

*T*his list is for people who do not already know the answer to the above question and is also good for people who do know because it will remind you of all the goodness you are supporting. Way to go! This is definite food for thought and are very important truths and facts! I have listed several sources, Websites and versions for your awareness and knowledge, please really think about what is happening and what all of our choices are supporting. Everyday we are actively shaping the world and reality all around us with each decision. With this fact in mind we can all consciously choose the best course of action for everyone and the world. That is why Rainbow Grocery is so great because they have already done all the figuring out and selected the best possible choices for you already, you can just relax and enjoy your shopping experiences there knowing you are doing and getting the best. Rainbow Grocery has lovingly taken a lot of care in choosing the best available organic products possible. So we can shop and enjoy knowing that with each dollar and choice we make that we are actively choosing and creating a world full of harmony, peace, joy and with a brighter future for everyone. Here is more great information:

> http://www.greenlivingnow.com
> http://www.greenlivingnow.com/children.htm

Here are ten more reasons to choose certified organic foods:

1. **Protect Future Generations**—Children receive 4 times the exposure of adults for at least 8 widely used cancer-causing pesticides in food. The food choices you make now will impact your child's health in the future.

2. **Prevent Soil Erosion**—The Soil Conservation Service estimates that more than 3 billion tons of topsoil is eroded from U.S. croplands each year. That means that soil is eroding 7 times faster than it is built up naturally. Soil is the foundation of the food chain in organic farming. In conventional farming, the soil is used more as a medium for holding plants in a vertical position while they are doused with synthetic chemical poisons and fertilizers.

3. **Protect Water Quality**—Water makes up two thirds of our body mass and covers three fourths of the planet. Despite its importance, the Environmental Protection Agency estimates that pesticides (some cancer causing) contaminate ground water in 38 states,

polluting the primary source of drinking water for more than half of the country's population.

4. **Save Energy** Modern farming uses more petroleum than any other single industry, consuming 12 percent of the country's total energy supply. More energy is now used to produce synthetic fertilizers than to till, cultivate, and harvest, all of the crops in the U.S. Organic farming is still based on labor-intensive practices, such as: weeding by hand, rotating crops, and green cover crops, rather than synthetic chemicals.

5. **Keep Chemicals Off Your Plate**—Many of the pesticides approved for use by the EPA were registered before extensive research linking these chemicals to cancer and other diseases had been established. Now the EPA considers that 60 percent of all herbicides, 90 percent of all fungicides, and 30 percent of all insecticides are carcinogenic. The bottom line is that pesticides are poisons designed to kill living organisms, including humans.

6. **Protect Farm Workers Health**—A National Cancer Institute study found that farmers exposed to herbicides had a 6 times greater risk than non-farmers of contracting cancer. In California, reported pesticide poisonings among farm workers have risen an average of 14 percent a year since 1973, and doubled between 1975 and 1985. Pesticides poison an estimated 1 million people annually.

7. **Help Small Farmers**—Most organic farmers are small in scale and 48 percent gross less than $15,000 per year. Join an organic community supported agriculture (CSA) group, and/or purchase from organic farmers at farmer's markets and farm stands.

8. **Support A True Economy**—The price of organic food represents the true cost of raising healthy food. Conventionally grown food does not reflect the hidden costs borne by taxpayers, like hazardous waste disposal and cleanups, environmental damage, pesticide regulation, health insurance hikes, etc. In 1988, nearly $14 billion in federal subsidies were given to conventional growers. Why?

9. **Promote Biodiversity**—Between 1950 and 1970, the practice of planting large plots of land with the same crop, year after year (monocropping), initially tripled farm production. The bad news is that this lack of diversity of plant life has left the soil lacking in natural minerals and nutrients. In an attempt to replace the nutrients and ward off the

increasing number of pests, chemical fertilizers and toxic pesticide use has increased. In fact, between 1947 and 1974, crop losses due to insects have doubled.

10. **Better Taste and More Nutrition**—Researchers from the University of Copenhagen recently reported that organically grown produce has higher levels of nutrients, like vitamins and secondary metabolites (which are thought to lower the risk of cancer) as compared to conventionally grown produce.

The following Website is from England, in Europe Organic Food has been normal and mainstream with the highest demand in the world.

http://www.villageorganics.com/whybuyorganic.html

1. **It's healthy**—On average, organic food contains higher levels of vitamin C and essential minerals such as calcium, magnesium, iron and chromium as well as cancer-fighting antioxidants.

2. **No nasty additives**—Organic food doesn't contain food additives which can cause health problems such as heart disease, osteoporisis, migraines and hyperactivity. Amongst the additives banned by the Soil Association are hydrogenated fat, aspartame (artificial sweetener) and monosodium glutamate.

3. **Avoids pesticides**—Over 400 chemical pesticides are routinely used in conventional farming and residues are often present in non-organic food. The UK government has recently found high levels of pesticide residues in baby food, spinach, dried fruit, bread, apples, celery, and chips.

4. **GM-free**—Genetically modified (GM) crops and ingredients are not allowed under organic standards.

5. **Reliance on drugs removed**—There is growing concern about the high use of antibiotics on farm animals and the possible effects on human health. Soil Association standards prohibit the routine use of antibiotics.

6. **No hidden costs**—Compare this with the £120m that tax payers fork out to pay for chemicals to be removed from drinking water, mainly as a result of the pesticides used in farming.

7. **High standards**—Organic food comes from trusted sources. All organic farms and foo-companies are inspected at least once a year. The standards for organic food are laid down in European law.

8. **Care for animals**—Animal welfare is taken very seriously under organic standards and is supported by animal rights organizations such as Compassion in World Farming as well as the UK government.

9. **Good for wildlife and the environment**—The UK government has said that it is better for wildlife, causes lower pollution from sprays, produces less carbon dioxide - the main global warming gas - and less dangerous wastes.

10. **Top for taste**—Researchers from the University of Copenhagen recently reported that organically grown produce has higher levels of nutrients, like vitamins and secondary metabolites (which are thought to lower the risk of cancer) as compared to convention-ally grown produce.

There is more information:

ENVIRONMENTAL REASONS:

Cleaner water and air

One of the main reasons people support organics is that they believe synthetic fertilizers, pesticides, herbicides and fungicides to be potentially toxic to our environment. Not only are they potentially toxic where they lie but they may also eventually work their way down to the water level polluting much of the drinking water. And when sprayed, pesticide residues are left in the air for all creatures to breathe. These residues unfortunately stay around while others are continually being added. Many take years, decades and sometimes even centuries to break down.

Healthier soil

Others believe that healthier soil and the prevention of soil erosion is a good reason to support organics. In organic gardening, the soil is built up and enriched through the use of organic material such as compost, much in the same way that Mother Nature provides nu-trients when she drops her leaves in the autumn, etc. Rather than depending on synthetic fertilizers which feed only the plant, the soil is actually fed so that our very earth becomes richer in nutrients and less prone to erosion. In addition, many organic growers routinely rotate their crops, plant cover crops and grow a more diverse range of plants on a particular plot of land. All of these practices help to conserve the minerals and nutrients in the soil.

Conserve water

Healthy, nutrient rich soils created through the practices of organic gardening also retain moisture more easily, reducing the need for additional watering.

Balanced ecosystem

There are still others that choose the effects on ecosystems as their basis for supporting organics. Though pesticides may kill a particular pest, eventually resistant strains can develop, ultimately creating an even more difficult pest control situation. Also in the process of aiming at a particular pest, competitors and natural enemies of other pests will inadvertently be killed off, leading to an increased population of other pests. It is also believed by some that many song birds have disappeared from our world, possibly because of, being at the top of a long food chain, they are ingesting highly concentrated doses of chemicals. These are just a few examples of how our ecosystem can be affected.

Conserve energy

Some believe that organic farming saves energy. They believe that it takes more energy to produce synthetic fertilizers than it does to cultivate, till and harvest crops. Also farms have changed so drastically over the years, from small, family based businesses that depend more on the energy of humans to large farm factories that depend on other forms of energy such as petroleum.

Increased bio-diversity

Because mono-cropping (the practice of planting the same crop on the same plot of land year after year) is less prevalent in organic farming, growing organically may help to preserve thousands of, otherwise lost, varieties of natural edible plants, ultimately providing us with a greater choice of fruits and vegetables.

Use of plants suited for environment

Organic growers generally use plants that are suited to their environment and disease resistant varieties therefore reducing the need for fertilizers, pesticides, herbicides and fungicides.

HEALTH REASONS:

Keep pesticides off our food and out of our bodies

Everytime we eat something that has been treated with a pesticide, let's say an apple, we are ingesting a government accepted low level of pesticide residue. And although research is conflicting and sometimes hard to weed through, many choose to buy organically grown food because they believe these residues to be potentially carcinogenic and perhaps even related to certain birth defects, nerve damage and genetic mutations. Also, some believe that pesticides are in higher concentrations the higher you go on the food chain. That is, "pesticides don't just affect the creature who ingests them first. They accumulate in the tissues of animals, and then, as one organism is eaten by another, they build up ever higher concentrations at each successfully higher rung on the chain." In addition, consumption of livestock, poultry and dairy products that contain hormones and growth stimulants may possibly play a role in the pre-mature development of children.

Most importantly, no one knows the effects of ingesting all of these various pesticide residues in combination with one another, nor do we know the long term effects of ingesting such pesticide residues and hormones over a period of a lifetime.

A healthier place to live

t is obvious that the health of our environment has a direct impact on our own personal health. Cleaner water to drink and air to breathe can only mean a healthier you.

Nutritious food

Healthier soil means a healthier plant. The healthy soil created through the process of organic gardening means soil full of nutrients. And soil full of nutrients means food rich in nutrients.

SOCIAL REASONS:

Safer conditions for workers

Because of the health risks involved when applying various pesticides, herbicides and fungicides, supporting organics will help provide for a safer working environment for field workers.

Support small business

About ten families eating organic food will support one small organic farm.

Leave a legacy for our children

Supporting organics will help to ensure a cleaner and healthier planet for generations to come.

More Great Websites

As a Raw Organic Gourmet Chef I have encountered a lot of different views about salt, so far the major agreement is that sea salt is beneficial and is good in moderation. Everyone has different and individual needs and should decide on their own, I do want to list some information that I found on the Internet about sea salt and to list more great Websites:

http://www.curezone.com/foods/saltcure.asp

In the theory of acid and alkaline balance, chronic disease such as cancer is caused by the acidification of the blood, lymph and all cellular tissues. Real sea salt is one of the basic elements necessary part to correct this problem.

http://www.truestarhealth.com/members/cm_archives14ML3P1A52.html

In fact, your body contains about four ounces of sodium, keeping your internal fluids in a state very similar to ocean water and this is absolutely critical for your body to function.

http://www.medical-library.net/sites/framer.html?/sites/_salt_addiction.html

If you use salt, use only sea salt, which contains all the other minerals your body needs in a balanced mixture, and use it sparingly.

Sodium *is* necessary for proper transmission of impulses along the axon of every nerve in your body, and necessary for muscle contraction as well. Deficiency of sodium is difficult to achieve, because sodium salts are everywhere in nature.

BY RON KENNEDY, M.D., SANTA ROSA, CALIFORNIA

The particular salt we refer to in human nutrition, unless otherwise specified, is sodium chloride. It is plentiful and cheap, but it wasn't always so conveniently available. Sodium chloride once was considered a great delicacy to be used sparingly because it was difficult to obtain and expensive. Roman soldiers of antiquity were often paid in salt, and this was called their "*salarium*," from which our word "salary" is derived. It was said a soldier was "worth his salt," a term still used for a worthy person. Once paid with salt, it could be used as money in exchange for other goods.

Sodium and potassium individually combine with bicarbonate, phosphorus or chlorine, to make the six major salts in the human body. Potassium and sodium are metals forming positive ions (cations, i.e., missing an electron) each with an electrical charge of +1. Phosphate, bicarbonate and chloride are negative ions (anions) with a negative charge of -1, having an extra electron. All these ions are found in the human body. In health, they all work together along with the kidneys to maintain the acid/base balance of the body within a very narrow, slightly alkaline range. Each cation is balanced by an anion, existing in an almost 1:1 ratio, with a slight excess of anions. Bicarbonate is a buffer, able to absorb and neutralize both acid and base, thus holding the acid/base balance within the narrow range necessary for life.

The concentration of these salts is very close to the concentration of the same salts found in ocean water, out of which our distant ancestors walked a few hundred million years ago to begin animal life on land. Our cells have maintained the memory of sea water from which our ancestors came.

http://www.Madhavahoney.com
http://www.g-forse.com/archive/news307_e.html Organic Athletes!
http://www.jhsph.edu/Environment/Get_Involved/2_health.html
http://ww1.mid-day.com/smd/eat/2003/november/68901.htm
http://www.beantrees.com/fr_main/why_GO_organic.htm
http://www.omorganics.com
http://www.sivananda.org
http://www.sfyoga.com
http://www.yogitimes.com
http://www.molokaiorganics.com
http://www.jacobsfarm.com
http://www.fresh-network.com
http://www.rainbow.coop
http://www.Extremehealthgoji.com
http://www.sfvs.org
http://www.onetastesf.com
http://www.healthybn.com

Some new people may find the word Raw to be a big barrier or a challenge to accept, we live in a cooked processed world, so to help overcome this stigma or new lifestyle I have come up with new descriptive terms for the Raw Organic Cuisine that is fun and can be used instead of saying Raw so that people can be more open and accepting of Raw:

High Vibrational Cuisine
Hallelujah Diet
Eden Diet

The way we ate for millions of years diet

Live-it Cuisine

Living Cuisine

True Blessing Meals

Pure Love Light Dining

Light Sunfood

Super Foods

No Heat to Eat Food

No Bake tastes Great Food

I hope everyone enjoyed the journey with me, there is much more goodness to come. I also hope that people will learn, share and teach others! Thank you and enjoy!

Printed on 100% recycled paper

ISBN 1-41205018-9

9 781412 050180